MARKETING, THE SACROSANCT MANTRA

MARKETING, THE SACROSANCT MANTRA

MVJAY

PARTRIDGE
A Penguin Random House Company

Copyright © 2014 by MVJAY.

ISBN:	Hardcover	978-1-4828-3763-6
	Softcover	978-1-4828-3762-9
	eBook	978-1-4828-3761-2

All rights reserved. No part of this book may be used or reproduced by any means, graphic, electronic, or mechanical, including photocopying, recording, taping or by any information storage retrieval system without the written permission of the publisher except in the case of brief quotations embodied in critical articles and reviews.

Because of the dynamic nature of the Internet, any web addresses or links contained in this book may have changed since publication and may no longer be valid. The views expressed in this work are solely those of the author and do not necessarily reflect the views of the publisher, and the publisher hereby disclaims any responsibility for them.

To order additional copies of this book, contact
Partridge India
000 800 10062 62
orders.india@partridgepublishing.com

www.partridgepublishing.com/india

Contents

Preface 9
Foreword 11

Chapter 1   Why this Book? 15
Chapter 2   Marketing- Is it the Sacrosanct Mantra of Public sector Banks in India? 20
Chapter 3   What is the difference between Marketing and Selling? 23
Chapter 4   Mistake at concept level ends as a mistake 32
Chapter 5   Why Marketing as a Vertical in Public Sector Banks 34
Chapter 6   Maintain the hierarchy 44
Chapter 7   Don't allow distraction 48
Chapter 8   Identification of market 52
Chapter 9   Let someone else do it 59
Chapter 10 Dearth of service in third party products leaves a bad impression 62
Chapter 11 Tech Savvy – be a real one 65
Chapter 12 Never be a launching pad always- also fly 69
Chapter 13 Unlearning and paradigm shift 72
Chapter 14 Concept delay and Concept dying 76

Chapter 15	Which is correct approach? Dogmatic or pragmatic	81
Chapter 16	Marketing is all Pervasive across the Pyramid	87
Chapter 17	Marketing and Technology are the interwoven twine of Banking	93
Chapter 18	Team Building: Who are members of the team? Whether individuals or departments. Who are the coordinators?	98
Chapter 19	Then what sales really is?	102
Chapter 20	Marketing strategy does not differentiate between people, cadre or hierarchy	104
Chapter 21	Subtle difference between Marketing and Corporate communication	107
Chapter 22	What are third party products and their impact on marketing	112
Chapter 23	"Play safe technique", the holy chant of Public Sector	116
Chapter 24	Cost determination, cost analysis and cost cutting are essential tools of Marketing	119
Chapter 25	Understanding the customer and Differential pricing technique are also marketing tools	121
Chapter 26	Product positioning is a strategy in banking parlance	126
Chapter 27	Shifting customers across various channels is also a marketing tool	130
Chapter 28	Segmentation, targeting and positioning – An understanding	134

Chapter 29	Innovation is not possible?	138
Chapter 30	Minimum pyramid hierarchy	141
Chapter 31	What are the missing links in public sector?	145
Chapter 32	Can SERVQUAL and GAP model help public sector?	149
Chapter 33	What requires to be done in public sector bank?	157

About the Author...163

Preface

"Marketing is the strategic process of deciding the price, product mix, customer and positioning of products and services by a business unit. "Sales" is the process of execution of the market plan evolved by the marketing activity. Marketing is more abstract in nature whereas Sales is more Physical or wholesome".

Public Sector Banks in India have created a vertical known as Marketing but the purpose of creating is not fulfilled as the marketing team is only engaged in physical selling activity. In other words, it is a mockery and euphemistic style of saying sales. Thus, Marketing is a sacrosanct mantra in Public Sector Banks in India. Having worked in marketing department for nearly a decade continuously, I noticed that there is a misconception about the concept of marketing in the minds of many employees in any Public Sector Units more so in the case of nationalized Banks. It is imperative that the subtle difference between Marketing and Sales should be understood by employees of any organization more specifically Public Sector Banks.

My intention is not to hurt any individual or organization while I reveal the intricacies in my Book. The readers should be able to differentiate between the two phrases so that they can effectively function without murmur or bickering. My effort in this book will be to make the reader understand that Marketing is strategic in nature whereas Sales is a process of execution. Marketing is more abstract in nature whereas Sales is more physical or wholesome. Marketing will not be complete in its function unless Sales takes place. My idea is not to disapprove the attempt of Public Sector Banks in introducing the Marketing Vertical. My concern is that whether that is effectively used. Even now there are attempts by some Banks, some senior marketing executives and senior officials to allocate retail sales task for junior marketing officers. There are attempts by them to sell medical insurance policies and credit cards in retail. For a Pan India Banking Institution deploying marketing official to sell products in retail is tantamount to selling products like cucumber or carrot in retail market. Some executives of marketing department fix targets for their marketing officers in retail selling without understanding to what extent they are wasting the man power. Having served a Public Sector Bank for more than 3 decades, I felt that I should convey the thoughts through this book. My only intention is to bring a paradigm shift in the thinking process on the subject Marketing, Sales and Technology with reference to Banking Industry. Marketing concept should permeate right from the sub ordinate cadre staff to the CMD level cadre in Public Sector Banks.

MVJAY

Foreword

Promoting sales and retaining customers are the twin objectives set to be carried out effectively by any successful corporate be it in the manufacturing or service sector, in pursuit of sustainable growth in a globally competitive market.

It is the responsibility of the marketing department in any business to draw out strategies pertaining to

1. Customer,
2. Products,
3. Markets &
4. Price.

and support the various activities in the supply chain to achieve set objectives.

The author has in a subtle manner brought out the inadequacies in marketing strategies of public sector banks and how this has affected the profitable performance of the banks in the process of reaching out to customers through the three types of products – Deposits, Credit and other services.

Lack of vision and creativity in designing a product and positioning it to attract the customers and mixing up the purpose of marketing and selling have pushed many valuable customers away from public sector banks to the private banks. The book highlights how the public sector banks have not fully exploited the advantages of the nuances available in using Information Technology tools to hover around any customer while serving him with any one of the products, be it in-house or third party.

The internecine quarrels between the IT, Corporate Communications and Marketing departments in trying to establish their prime position in the organization hierarchy and how this has blurred the internal channels of communication are vividly explained in this book. The author highlights the importance of creativity in the design, development and positioning of any product to a customer and the need to give full freedom to the marketing department and top management support to pursue their marketing goals. The imperative of empowering officials in the branches in handling the products offered to customers and the follow up mechanism to retain the customer in the bank fold are nicely brought out in the book.

Effective communication both internal and external holds the key in reaching out to the customers. It is rightly said that if the language is not correct what is said is not what is meant. If what is said is not what is meant what ought to be done remains undone.

The global mantra is to provide cost effective products and services to the customers. In choosing the product positioning strategies the marketing department should lay emphasis on the importance of monitoring cost. In deploying a differentiation strategy the guiding factor should be the inclusion of unavoidable cost of differentiation. A customer does not like to pay for any non value adding service by the bank – a point well brought out.

The father of the Indian Nation, Mahatma Gandhi is right in saying that the customer is the most important person in our premises. He gives us business and should treat him as God. Customer irrationality is a very important psyche and getting into that calls for quality service.

This book can be an eye opener for bank officials who can add value to their activities and help the nationalized banks to turn around and be competitive.

A. Madhavan B.Com; FCMA

Director,

ACQUALIB CORPORATE SERVICES PRIVATE LIMITED, CHENNAI, INDIA.

1

Why this Book?

"Here the coordination is between the various departments of banking, more particularly marketing, technology and sales (field level branch)". It is nothing but analogy of supply chain management principle in banking industry.

All Nationalized banks give more interest on deposits to their customers, charge less for the services offered to the customers and charge lesser rates for the loans and advances given to the customers. These banks' charges are lesser when compared to new generation banks and private banks. These banks give the best redress mechanisms to the customers and the banks as a whole are approachable from the lowest official to the top executive of the bank.

On the other hand the new generation banks or the private banks give lesser rate of interest for the deposits at times for the public, they relatively levy more service charges & ad hoc charges for the services extended and they charge more interest for the loans and advances. They also have redress mechanism mostly through the IVR. The main difference between these new generation/private banks and the government banks is the human touch or the availability of human response for the customer when they need.

All sorts of complaints and grievances are taken for consideration by the public sector banks. Relevant complaints are taken by the new generation/private banks. Still why the customer prefers the new generation/private bank? The fact is that the new generation/private banks maintain their supply chain management intact. The co ordination between the various departments, the continuity of service & chronology of service, chronologically updating the terms of service attuning to the present trend in the banking industry and making the customer satisfied with the supply of what is wanted by him is being done by these banks.

The issue with the public sector banks is that there is no coordination between the various departments. In many occasions the website may be showing some interest rate or service charges and the branch will be charging different rate or service charges. In effect, the supply chain management circle is not completed possibly so that the customer is not inclined to glue himself with the public sector banks always. Whenever and wherever the charges or services are ok and acceptable the customer stays with the bank and leaves the bank the moment he is dissatisfied.

The new generation banks/private banks try to meet the requirement of the generation "Y" and try to give their best service at the door step. They give the option for the younger generation to stay away from the bank premises. This is not possible for the public sector banks. Right from opening the account to operations of the account, the new generation customer would be required to be present in banks' premises which they resent. When such customer makes his presence amongst difficulties, the branch/bank official will not be available; whatever is the reason.

The new generation banks understand the customers, their requirement, as long as they know and estimate that further business is possible from them. A potential customer of new generation bank can without any instrument like cheque or demand draft get few lakhs of rupees delivered at his residence or airport in case of acute emergency for which the banks also oblige. This will never happen in a public sector bank under normal circumstances. Customers would like an air ticket to be delivered at the airport by the branch manager of a new generation/private bank. This would never happen with the public sector bank.

Thanks to Mr. Keith Oliver who introduced the principle of supply chain management. It had been very relevant in any business including banking industry too. Amongst the commonly accepted definitions of supply chain management let us take the following.

A banker, an intelligent banker; while bringing customer to the bank, would meet an elderly customer, probably a senior citizen, an average aged person, a budding youth and children. The senior citizen would come with his retired funds, might require in addition to his SB/pension account, some remittance facility or some insurance schemes. The average aged person would like to have in addition to his SB account, some mutual funds scheme, pension related insurance schemes, health insurance schemes, educational loan for his son or daughter and so on. The budding youth will be requiring a vehicle loan in addition to his salary account, some remittance facility to his parents, credit card, educational loan for higher studies, home loan and insurance of all types etc. A kid's account might require an ATM card, fee remittance facility and so on. The banker's interest should be more on bringing the last two types. It does not mean the banker should discard or casually treat the top two types. The supply chain management principle advocates the banker to go in for the first decision.

The endeavour is to create customer satisfaction at the end point of delivery to the consumer. As a consequence, costs must be lowered throughout the chain by driving out unnecessary expenses, movements, and handling. The main focus is turned to efficiency and added value or the end-user's perception of value. Efficiency must be increased, and bottlenecks removed. Here again the thought of pushing the customers across the various channels comes into picture. **This is meticulously done by the new generation banks/private bank.**

Finally very importantly, the systematic, strategic coordination of traditional business functions and tactics across all business functions within the supply chain, for the purposes of improving the long-term performance of the individual bank and the supply chain as a whole is required. **Here the coordination is between the various departments of banking, more particularly marketing, technology and sales (field level branch). It is nothing but analogy of supply chain management principle in banking industry.**

The tactics is cost reduction and customer retention. Many of the public sector banks in India are century old. **Have they all applied the principle of supply chain management effectively as the new generation/ private banks have applied?** At least now onwards the managements should think of applying this principle and recoup the lost clientele by synergizing the available resources of man power.

2

Marketing- Is it the Sacrosanct Mantra of Public sector Banks in India?

"<u>My aim in writing this book is not to chide the attempt of Public sector Banks but to make the reader understand how various Banks view marketing.</u>"

Public sector banks created a vertical known as Marketing but the effect of it was not great. For namesake, the department was created and it was more or less a mockery and **euphemistic reference to Sales.** Thus Marketing became a sacrosanct Mantra of public sector banks in India. More and more public sector banks had created the vertical in Marketing but none of them were very clearly able to define the exact functions of marketing department. Some banks had defined the role and responsibility of marketing department for name sake. The actual work assigned to marketing department would be different. The officials in marketing department would be engaged in varying activities as per requirements of the senior executives and would be more or less doing the job of Public Relations Officer of banks. Banks had been recruiting MBAs of leading business schools like IIMs and experienced marketing officers from various other industries to serve marketing department. But some questions stare at our face.

- Had they defined the functions of marketing department correctly?

- Had these banks effectively formulated a scheme in which those officers could be used effectively?

- Would there be any mileage out of these specialist officers and what would be the output of the marketing department as a whole?

Readers of this book might be customers; youngsters; ex bankers, current bankers, marketing department officials of Public or Private sector bank or Government officials. **My aim in writing this book is not to disapprove the attempt of Public Sector Banks but to make the reader understand how various Banks view marketing.** Executives of various banks per se attach different meanings for the word marketing. Readers should also understand the limitations of the marketing officers of public sector banks. The reader would be able to appreciate the situations under which marketing officials worked in Public sector banks in comparison with the Private bank peers. Many readers would wonder when there was a possibility of a Private bank opening a SB account so simply why Public sector bank sat on more formalities. How a Private sector bank marketing official could assure a loan so easily by himself and clearly make it available when a marketing official of Public sector bank was unable to assure the same and Public sector bank took time to issue such loans with lots of **ifs and buts**? Why private sector banks had clarity on products whereas public sector did not have that much clarity? The reader would appreciate, after reading this book, why a private sector marketing official was able to extend a clearly defined service within stipulated time whereas the public sector marketing man was unable to talk clearly on services. The reader would come to know the functionality and powers and understandings in public sector. Then only he would get to know the real position of officials especially marketing officials in Public sector banks.

3

What is the difference between Marketing and Selling?

"The Banks should have created a sales department with a sales force for the vision they had. Instead all the banks created a vertical called marketing department, thereby jeopardizing the bank as well as the individual who had real marketing capability"

When I was posted to a branch initially, I sold my self to the clerical and sub ordinate staff and then with the officer cadre staff too. By that time, I was going on tours. I could contact similar officers and clerks from various banks. We used to share our views, ideas and business details. Whomever I contacted said "I have sold 10 policies", "I have sold 20 policies", "I have sold 20 gold coins", "I have sold 100 MF units" etc.

There used to be meetings arranged by these Mutual fund companies and the Insurance companies for us to encourage us and see that we at the least stayed with selling process. Banks had then started changing the nomenclature for the deposits, loans & services and each service or deposit or loan accounts were defined as products. That was easy for the management to apportion work to the officers who had come to marketing department. It was nice to know about the new nomenclature of the banking service but while doing so the nomenclature of making the product reach public namely marketing was not correctly done by any bank. The Banks should have created a sales department with a sales force for the vision they had. Instead all the banks created a vertical called marketing department, thereby jeopardizing the bank as well as the individual who had real marketing capability.

Some senior managers of PSBs then were repeatedly telling their marketing officers that they should market insurance policies. My manager also was repeatedly telling me that I should market the insurance policies. Just as my other inquisitive friends who had retorted, "Who would sell the products then?" I also asked my manager eventually who would sell them. Pat came the reply. In banking parlance marketing and selling meant the same. He also asked me back who else would sell these policies. I had to take up the matter with my zonal manager. He quietly asked, "What bothers you if the meaning is different". He said whether it was selling activity or marketing activity the ultimate action would be that the target business should be reached.

Then my turn came and I said that the business can come both by Selling and Marketing. Then my executive retorted, "What is marketing and selling in your words?"

I sat firmly unperturbed and replied, "any attempt to make known to the public that a product or service

MARKETING, THE SACROSANCT MANTRA

exists with the bank is marketing activity. Marketing activity defines the products like cakes or pizzas and puts them into the minds of customers for making them to buy. It is for the branch to sell the same. Marketing is the processes of making the customers know that the products available with the bank are superior and are varied and comparatively cheaper than others or competitively priced. Selling is the process by which the branch transferred the product given by the marketing department to the customer. The product which is lying with the branch will be transferred to the customer and that activity will be selling". The executive gave a crack jawed laugh and finished the argument saying, "call it by any name, but at the end of the day let us reach the target". I jovially said, "Sir, shall we suggest to change the name of our department as sales department?"

I used to take classes for various categories of clerks, junior and senior officers (not executives) on the topic of selling third party products. I had an occasion to take class for marketing officers alone and I was firm that I should differentiate between four concepts to them which would make them understand what was meant by marketing department per se. The headings were: Marketing, Selling, Cross selling and up selling. I felt these topics were well received by the officers and that would have given them some encouragement when they were posted to branches. They would have understood the reality with the bank.

That made me to explore the meaning of marketing in Public Sector Banks. Nearly for 10 years I had been associated with the marketing department. Till my last day I was unable to convince my superiors that both these functions were different. Whenever review of the marketing department would be held, the first question that would be raised would be "what is it marketing department has done or performed?". Mostly this question would be asked by the new incumbent General Manager and the team with Chief Manager or AGM would have an embarrassment to give a reply. The easy question that would be innocently put forward by the executive would be how many home loans, credit cards, ATM cards and insurance policies had been sold by the marketing department officials. The drama would continue further stating that the individual officers should be given a target for each category and performance monitored. It would be commented that Marketing Officers were whiling away their time.

By then some important domestic errand for the organization say, taking care of the MPs team or Ministry Officials would crop in and the first to be disturbed would be the marketing guys. My Keralite friend used to say, "Anna, we are like decorated elephants and we have to stand elegantly and enhance the show." I used to admire him always since his remarks only made me to sustain the pressure from the top management. He used to say, "Anna, if you throw the cat, it only falls on four feet". It took many months for me to understand the English version of this Malayalam proverb. Whenever I used to get dejected in front of the executive I used to think of this proverb and console me. Then how to make them understand our position?

Management decisions in many Public Sector Banks to go in for fresh Management students from leading institutions, ignoring the functional expertise of serving senior officials came a cropper in many banks, throwing the new recruits to mundane jobs. The new Mantra was "MBA students". **When job seekers had to attend competitive exams and come victorious among lakhs of aspirants, this method of recruiting youngsters in the name of marketing even though looked funny looked illogical also.** The paradoxical comedy was that these marketing Arjuns after a period of 2 or 3 years left their bow and arrow and switched over quietly to normal banking thereby depriving of the one in a million citizens who had gone through the process of competitive exams and got rejected. Why such sudden shift? It was obvious that those marketing professionals were asked to come out with their output produced. That might have made them to feel insecure, jittery and slowly, except one or two, others would have changed their loyalties to general banking. They clearly expressed that they were unable to distinguish between marketing and selling. Whatever they gave as their performance would have already been given by the branch manager as the target achieved. Then where else they would go for showing performance. Again the concept of marketing and selling would enter the area. Those MBAs, who would have come with some new ideas of marketing activity, would have failed to convince the top brass about their marketing proposals. To be in good books they would have accustomed to their executive's way of functioning. Thus they would stop emphasizing on marketing strategy and accept the target given for performance. Unable to perform they would drift to general category at the appropriate time.

The IIT/IIM concept then entered into Public sector banks. Suddenly the recruiting driving wheel turned its direction towards IIT/IIMs. Many students from these institutes then found charm in banking career and joined banks. Management could not decide the way in which they should be used. They were fish out of water without knowledge of basic banking and the intricacies of Indian way of banking.

Management could not also use them in prime area due to dearth of knowledge. They must have had their own hesitation to use these MBAs in top management decision making process. To the extent I had interacted with those guys I only found that they struggled to fit in to the mechanism of Public Sector. The systems and procedures sitting pretty over the novelty made them to disassociate with the general current. Some executives tried to use them in a better way, but many found them to be nagging than accommodating. This was my gut feeling after interaction with both sides.

PRISM effect always played a role here. Just because the top brass like CMD or ED had evinced sudden interest in these MBAs and IIMs the just promoted executives namely AGMs or DGMs started excessively commending and patting these new generation Babus without understanding their skills correctly. In crucial meetings the senior officials would be sidelined and these IIM chicks would be highlighted by AGM or DGM to a great extent thinking the top brass would relish that.

What was in the mind of these youngsters? God only would have known it precisely. But one thing was sure. They did not have any great idea about any one. Some had even got annoyed over the systems and procedures which had not given them free hand to test the waters.

Different jargons in Marketing and Selling

With all these things explained, have we defined marketing and selling? Especially with reference to the Public Sector banks?. Till today this will be an interesting topic for discussion. I will say six jargons with reference to public sector banks based on its activities. They are 1] Marketing 2] Selling 3] Cross Selling 4] Up selling 5] Vertical Selling and 6] Horizontal Selling.

Marketing is the process of bringing to the mind of the customers the existence of different products of the bank either by advertisements or through brochures or through digital displays.

Selling is the process of transferring the product from the bank's hand to the customer's hand.

Marketing is the process of bringing the customers to the bank for seeing the various products.

Selling is the process of putting any one of the products on his basket.

But this is not seriously understood or implemented by any Public Sector Bank. For them target is for all, be it branch manager, regional manager, zonal manager or marketing manager. How will these target overlap? That is immaterial. The total business target for the zone and overall for the bank should be reached, then everything would be forgotten. To show the performance of marketing department, often corporate communication activities and marketing activities would be clubbed and intermingled thereby losing the importance on both sides.

Cross selling is the process of selling extra products to the existing customer. When a customer comes to take a home loan giving the customer an insurance product is cross selling. Similarly selling gold coin to an existing customer is cross selling.

Up selling is the process of especially selling a higher value product to a customer who has already taken product with the Bank. Sanctioning a home loan to a customer who is already having RD account or FD account is a sort of up selling.

Horizontal selling means selling or cross selling products to the customer who have entered the bank's branch.

Vertical Selling means going to an organization or an institution and residential areas and selling bank's product to the people there.

At this juncture **I would like to coin two more Jargon** namely 1] **Horizontal Marketing** and 2] **Vertical Marketing.**

MARKETING, THE SACROSANCT MANTRA

In banking parlance Horizontal Marketing means the marketing techniques used by the branch staff and manager in selling the bank's product to the customers. Any attempt by any staff of the branch can be brought under this. It may be a strategy, stall activity, campaign or contest locally arranged. It revolves around the branch and its location and it does not or need not involve a great policy, system or procedure.

In banking parlance Vertical Marketing is a term used to mean marketing techniques used by the branch staff or manager in selling bank's product to outsiders, namely different corporate, business houses, Students of schools, colleges and Institutes either by serving them at their premises or at melas conducted at their premises or on meetings held at their complexes or premises with specific products to suit them. For example the manager of a bank may introduce a fees collection module to the students of a specific institute and request all students to utilize the services.

Many top officials in PSBs do not appreciate and understand the vital role played by the marketing team in reaching to different customers. Marketing efforts to open up the minds of the customer is the beginning of selling efforts that are required.

4

Mistake at concept level ends as a mistake

"B + (be positive) blood will never match up with A- (a negative) blood. The RH (Retaliating Habit - give as good as you get) factor will not work effectively between the seniors and the Young Turks."

Vertical Marketing and Marketing Vertical are different concepts by themselves. This has to be understood very clearly. In epic Ramayana, Sita insisted on existence of golden deer. Rama being Himself Lord, conceptually made a mistake to go after the golden deer, of course to educate and teach us and the end result was a mistake. "Any act with concept level mistake turns out to be a mistake by itself". Any organization has to define marketing as a concept and any conceptual mistake will end as a mistake. Any amount of inducting MBAs or IITs or IIMs would not do well if there is no clear marketing concept. B + (be positive) blood will never match up with A- (a negative) blood. The RH (Retaliating Habit - give as good as you get) factor will not work effectively between the seniors and the Young Turks. These MBAs, IITs and IIMs unless molded at the administrative levels

MARKETING, THE SACROSANCT MANTRA

of Top Management, will lose their sheen and will look miserable over the years. Recruiting them with good bait of assuring intellectual posting and using them for counters, pass book printing and to do errands would not only jeopardize the bank but demotivate the aspiring youngster. If the youngster understands the nuances of adjusting to the public sector psychology then greater will be the loss for both the organization and self.

There was a sudden thought concept of right person for the right job in corporate world. It should be the duty of any management to put the right person to the right job especially to marketing department. Let him be an MBA from any IIT or IIM or simply an experienced dedicated old horse like bank officer, if the right person with right attitude for marketing is posted to marketing department then it will strengthen the PSUs to gain a competitive advantage in positioning their products.

What will be a better idea after having recruited them for marketing department? The top brass should not hesitate to leave the job to youngsters. They know what is marketing and what is required for the bank. A top level supervision would be sufficient. Handing over them to mute or inept junior executives like AGMs or CMs in the name of marketing officers and asking them to do unprofessional work would only be waste of labour and money. The junior executives thinking that they can handle effectively these young ones, by not assigning them creative work, simply spoil their enthusiasm and zeal.

5

Why Marketing as a Vertical in Public Sector Banks

"A marketing officer should have a level playing field in which he can take his own parties and his own decisions of course fixing the responsibilities for his decisions."

Why Marketing was formed as a vertical in public sector banks. No one particular reason could be attributed to this. Originally, when the concept started, it meant all marketing strategies and activities. All officials in marketing department should involve in data collection on the locality, know the market share of their branch, know the requirement of the public in that particular area, analyze the various segments like industries, industrial workers, entrepreneurs, salaried personnel, household sector etc. He should hold survey in that area and ascertain the product palette. He should collect feedback on the products and suggest suitable modifications to the management. He should be able to arrange for campaigns and melas. In other words there should be both horizontal and vertical marketing/selling.

MARKETING, THE SACROSANCT MANTRA

Horizontal marketing/selling is making the walk-in customers to take our banks product.

Vertical marketing /selling is going to other organizations or business areas to market/sell our products. The marketing officer should be able to do both these types and help the manager to reach his target.

The size and strength of marketing department has been right from small size of three or four officials to the macro size of 200 to 300 officials. In most of these cases the idea to have formed the vertical would have been only to assist the branch manager to expand his business without interfering in the day to day branch routine.

Then the conflict between the branch manager and marketing officer comes. The marketing officer has to do the marketing activity for the branch manager, be it a stall, campaign or canvassing. Once the activity is over, then the manager claims it as his performance. Marketing manager has to give his performance appraisal to top management through the manager only. Then how the branch manager will give credit to the marketing officer for the performance? After all it is his target and performance for the branch. Thus the conflict begins.

There is no clear demarcation about the shares of the marketing officer and branch official in a particular assignment. If there is a clear cut demarcation by the management itself that the effort would be shared as 30: 70 or 20:80, then the conflict would not arise. Similarly if the management gives credit for the marketing activity alone to the marketing officer and the selling credit to the branch manager then also there would not any conflict.

There are certain occasions where the marketing officer would have brought a customer to the branch manager for any product. That product could be sold to the customer only if the branch manager is satisfied about the customer. The marketing officer might have evaluated the customer as per market position. But the branch manager might not do so. He may even ask for an account to be opened and to become branch customer first. He may also say that all his transactions/accounts should be transferred to his branch first from other bank and then only he can consider selling the product. Or the sanctioning authority may not lie in his hand. In such cases where is the question of fixing the target for the marketing manager. **When the activity of the Marketing officer depends on the decision making capability of the branch manager, then the marketing officer cannot achieve his target.** For sanction of any loan there should be branch manager's recommendations. If the marketing officer has to expect always the mercy of the branch manager, then fixing target on general assumption of work load would not encourage the marketing officer.

A marketing officer should have a level playing field in which he can take his own leads (parties) and his own decisions, of course fixing the responsibilities for his decisions. The marketing officer should alternatively be given marks for his marketing activity and for conversion of the marketing activity namely selling activity both he and the branch manager should take shared stake.

What then will be a suitable pattern for a marketing vertical especially in an Indian Public Sector Bank? Suppose the bank is networked as zones and then as branches, for each zone there should be one AGM/chief manager level in charge under whom 3 senior managers would work. Under each senior manager there would be Asst Mgr/Mgr level officers. The low cadre officers will be in such proportions so that at each stage one officer i.e. Manager or Asst Manager will have 5 branches under him for which he will be conducting the marketing activities. These officers will report to the senior managers in turn who will report to CM/AGM. These zones will in turn inform the Corporate /Head office marketing department which should contain Asst Mgrs, Mgrs, Chief Manager, AGM and GM. This team will report to ED who will finally take up the matter with CMD. Each Senior Manager/MGR/Asst MGR should be able to take care of three to five zones depending upon the activities of the zones.

This set up should clearly demarcate the core marketing activities like campaigns, stalls, road shows, spot activities. These members of various zonal teams would assist the branch to garner business through sheer marketing activities. These would not be defined as selling activities. These would be specific marketing activities. The selling effect would be given to the branch only.

How then the marketing officer would be evaluated? It would be based on the leads he is generating, the business potential he is creating, the impact he is creating through his campaigns, stall activities, road shows and spot activities. These officials should get a feedback sheet duly filled in by the customers attending these marketing activities. These officers can take up direct marketing, horizontal marketing and Vertical marketing. The evaluation of the feedback from the participants for all the above activities would be done in total and the officer would be rated.

What is the advantage of this rating? The officials acting for marketing will precisely know what is required out of them. There will not be conflict within the organization. The management will resort to the use of management by objectives for rating marketing activities. Marketing goals will be set and a measurement mechanism put in place to evaluate actual performance. These norms will be periodically tested and analyzed and the marketing activities will be classified in different patterns so as to achieve the organization goals and targets. The vertical thus created will co ordinate with the branches and zonal offices and compare the targets vis a vis their performance at given intervals of time.

In 1950 Peter F Drucker said that a marketing activity should bring customers in to its organization and such customers would bring automatically business into organization. Thus the aim of any marketing officer should be to improve client base from the lowest level of product which will develop into potential customer base in future.

Marketing the neglected department

Marketing Department happens to be the most neglected department in many of the public sector banks. In many banks the department will be allotted mostly to the executive who is on the verge of retirement. It may be junior level executive or senior level executive. Those executives will also hold ceremonious meetings with the staff of marketing department and will never be able to take any useful decisions or guidance. Such executives would dilly dally any decision especially which involves financial sanction fearing of smooth retirement. This may not be the case with all banks, but it happens with most banks.

A junior level executive will accept any proposal submitted to him by a subordinate marketing officer who has passed the proposal. Senior executive will accept any proposal which is to be passed by his junior executives. When there is a curt situation that the decision has to be taken by themselves, they would form executives' committee and put the ball to the committee. There also the proposal would be vetted by the junior executives only. This is not at all a healthy practice since marketing is an activity which does not bear immediate fruition. The marketing strategy takes time to work and a good implementation program is required for it. It encompasses Marketing Analysis, Marketing planning, Implementation and Control. A marketing thought should be developed for the organization as a whole. Marketing should be understood as a concept and Management function involving Product/Services, Production, Sales and

Marketing orientation towards the branch ultimately. Any service extension, price formulation, price discrimination (say for combo loan products- special rate of interest), differential pricing, promotional pricing should all be done by marketing department with the help of the Administrative layer in the Pyramid. Marketing department should be used to formulate creative and imaginative campaigning tools with all mediums including the face book. Constant evaluation of these campaigning tools or communicative tools should be reviewed periodically to suit the overall marketing strategy. Giving a radio campaign and not alerting the branches about the radio campaign would only embarrass the customers who, when visiting the branch, were turned down by the branch manager or front line staff. When the marketing department would bring in a proposal which was of sizable amount, the other executives would chide the department saying "what is the worth of the proposal."

Also many other departments very easily would shift their work to marketing department quoting some reason or other. Marketing department since generally headed by a weak executive would accept all such donkey's job of the organization and do bull work. Generally, Public-relations department, corporate Communications Department and development department's work would be passed on to marketing department knowingly or unknowingly.

The executive posted to marketing department should lead from the front and also uphold the credibility of his department by his sheer dedication and personal demeanour. In an instant case, it was surprising to note that an executive who was insisting that all the staff should hold bank's credit card, wanted to go in for a foreign bank's credit card. The reason for the same was that his bank's credit card was worthless. (Also he would have thought that staff might not respect him after his retirement because of his selfish mentality and attitude while serving as an executive). It was reported that he was heading the card section for quite some time but what was the impression he had left behind?. Another executive who used to chide any staff who tried to take home loan from other organization, on the verge of his retirement sought a loan for his sons from a foreign bank.

Amidst such persons, it was also seen that a good number of executives had taken pains to impress upon customers even when they had retired, to take the products of their bank. Those executives would have definitely during their tenure done justice to their department viz a viz the dubious executives.

Generally any BM or officer of a branch would not believe or take it for granted any new customer voluntarily entering his branch. If some staff, thinking that he was doing some marketing for the bank, recommended a customer that would be more disastrous. More doubts would come to the branch manager. BM would like to take staff's name in the records somewhere in the corner to mean on a later date that the staff was the one who arranged the party. Similarly, when a staff recommended a loan, then BM would like to register a lien in the name of the staff too. When the party stopped payment to loans, BM would hold the staff responsible. Similarly when a retired staff would bring a party, the entire branch staff would doubt his intentions.

Similarly, some of the executives would pamper some parties who were not evaluated by the marketing team as worthy. Even though these executives knew that such parties would become NPA or would not be prompt in repaying the loans, there would be a possibility of extending some huge loans to such parties. The executives might, after retirement, take up some important positions in those organizations. Their attitude would definitely damage the innocent marketing department staff. They would feel they were neglected and their views were neglected. More would be felt by them when they saw the account slipping to poor category.

When executives got posted to marketing department, due to personal vengeance, they would chide the previous executive and sarcastically pass on comments about them and demean officers who were praised by the earlier one. This would happen due to the fact that there did not exist a structured activity for the department and any activity would have been due to the whimsical fancies of the executive who had held the position prior to this executive.

To make the marketing department more dependable and make it a department not neglected by any one down the lane, the only idea is to bring it under the control of the top executive or CEO/CMD or at least

ED so that everyone down the lane would regard marketing department.

The top management committee which is the administrative committee should define the nature of marketing department. For execution of the idea, the middle management and GM level executives should be used. Unless a senior level executive heads the department, the relevance of marketing activity would be lost and most of the down the lane executives and officers would never see the subtle difference between the two functions namely marketing and selling. It is to be noted that a perfect communication system is very much required for the bank as a whole.

6

Maintain the hierarchy

"It should be emphatic and clear from the desk of top management that no official in the line management violates the hierarchy. This will avoid lower officials like DGM or Zonal Managers demanding work from senior corporate/head office officials using the name of CEO/CMD/ED."

When a hierarchy is fixed it should be strictly followed. If the information has to flow from CMD>> ED >> GM>> DGM>> AGM>> ZM>>MKTG –in-Charge Zone>> Sr MGR >> MGR/Asst MGR, it should run in that flow.

In many public sector banks, there may be clash of same cadre executives in certain levels which will affect severely marketing activity. It should be seen that all zones are headed by one cadre less than the top cadre in Corporate/Head office. It means if ED is head of marketing then all zones can be of GM. If GM is head of marketing then it will be better if the zonal managers are of DGM cadre. This may not always be possible but it is advantageous.

MARKETING, THE SACROSANCT MANTRA

What happens when the marketing department and zonal manager happen to be in same cadre? The zonal manager who is senior will assign marketing activities to the GM in Head Office/corporate office. When MD/ED interacts with the GMs of Zones and insists on performance, then GMs of Zones would say they have lots of contact but do not have sufficient manpower. This is one way of escapism. MD/ED would definitely say, "Get those details, our marketing team will look into it." The job of GM/Zone is over and he sits comfortably and insists on performance of corporate/ Head office. The hierarchy is lost and the motivation gets lost over these activities. If it is one cadre less then at least the DGM would think twice before giving such work to corporate office/ Head office. MD/EDs should also avoid such situations. There may be smart DGMs who are handpicked chicks of top brass. They may also be able to get things done like this. For effective marketing, there should a crystal clear hierarchy system followed.

It is nothing wrong in doing the work of the zone but if all the zones adopt this strategy to jettison their work, then marketing department might have to increase its strength enormously. Similarly when accepting the task of the zones, it is to be remembered that the marketing officials of the corporate office would be devoid of all the facts that would be available only to those marketing or development officials present in the zonal office. Those in zones would know the demography, field, market forces, imbalances and quality and talent of our team.

Assuming that the corporate office marketing official is capable of making headway with one of the addresses from the list given by zone, then he has to make a contact and interaction. The needs of the customers are to be assessed by him and making an estimate he has to contact again the zone only since the power of pushing the papers through any branch does not lie in his hand. He has to make the proposal and put it through the zone. Again the process starts at zonal level. In the meantime, any other smart public or private sector bank would sanction the loan and snatch the customer from previous bank's hold.

It is to be noted at this juncture that even though this work first emanated from zonal office, after the proposal is followed by head office or corporate office and then pushed to the Zones, zonal officials would not see the proposal as their own. They would apply all doubts about the proposal and delay the proposal. In Indian Public sector bank, it is noted with pain that some good proposals which will add value to the bank do not see the light of the day due to lack of consensus between different officials due to departmental rancor. In such a situation the possibility of examining the proposal using rigorous norms and procedures creeps in due to personal animosity, thereby sidelining the main benefits that may accrue to the organization.

Who should see and maintain the hierarchy?

It should be emphatic and clear from the desk of top management that no official in the line management violates the hierarchy. This will avoid lower officials like

DGM or Zonal Managers demanding work from senior corporate/head office officials using the name of CEO/CMD/ED.

Once the hierarchy is maintained, the review of performance becomes fair and justifiable. This will help discharge of functions by the officials in the corporate office to add value to the bank and avoid unnecessary conflict of interest and non value adding efforts at both levels, i.e. corporate office and the zones. This will also send clear signals to the zonal people to avoid circumventing corporate level officials in getting favours from the CEO/CMD. In the event of continuous violation of hierarchy, the head office officials who perform under pressure may get into a negative mode and multiply work by involving unsolicited zones. They would try to leave their original work and indulge in helping the other zone's officials. In this process, the line of activity will be lost and productivity will get reduced to a great extent. A clear organization chart showing the delegation of powers, viz a viz the roles and responsibilities of the officials at different levels, should be made operational and binding on the erring executives with suitable punishments. This will facilitate smooth flow of work in the marketing department and help to boost the business at all levels.

7

Don't allow distraction

"The bane of marketing department is that all top executives would always like to chide the department stating that they are always loitering without doing any work."

I had heard from my colleagues from other banks that officers of various departments would take up typing work of clerks thereby not allowing clerks to do their duty. Why this should happen? The officers were in excess of their requirement. When their higher officials saw them sitting idle they would get annoyed and might think there were excess officers. To avoid this situation, the officers would pluck that portion of work which involves typing work also. They would never give typing work to the clerks back, go on typing the matter by themselves with the result whenever the executive saw them they were always engaged in work. The clerks would also feel this comfortable quite naturally. Why this attitude? This is called distraction. The executives, be it in Development, HRM, Accounts or Marketing or any other section, would like to have always reserve staff whenever they have emergencies.

They would impress up on the top management and would love to retain more staff for their department. Especially, Planning, HRM, Accounts, Agri finance and credit division would have more staff. However this would hurt the HRM department and when discussion comes on staff strength, the top executive would be convinced that these departments should be given more staff. Executives of that department would also advise their staff to show to outside world that there was sufficient work in their department.

When many departments had the phenomena, it is a fancy in PSUs to dig at the marketing department with the remark that the officials have inadequate or sometimes no work. This will dissuade the head of the marketing team to pursue any proposal for manpower increase even if the work pressure warrants, due to fear of being criticized by other peers. Some junior executives at times would be cleverer enough to take some other department's work in their fold and show that they had done something. For example, the allied work like corporate communication, MIS related work and development activities would be grabbed from those departments and marketing department would be doing those jobs so that when the top executives wanted to know about the job roles, the junior executive say - AGM or chief manager would have sufficient performance to boast of. In other words, the marketing department may be doing odd and menial jobs without adding any value to the bank.

Why this happened? The junior executive would be incapable of convincing the top executive about the intensity of marketing activities and to convince also that marketing activities could not itself have any quantifiable measure. Marketing activity had been successful wherever the top executive had felt that it was a strategic work and no target could be fixed for marketing activities. The marketing strategies should increase selling for which targets could be fixed. Instead of convincing the top executive about the quality of marketing activities, the junior executives would take on distraction tactics to escape. **The top executive should understand this and give freedom to the Marketing department to chalk out a programme which would set selling activity on motion.** It should be emphasized that quantum of sales and marketing strategies should have some bearing so that the marketing department would co ordinate with the sales department (branches) to improve business. Junior Executives who accept/grab other department's work for filling time should be in fact discouraged and warned that it may affect their promotion in the organization.

As far as marketing department is concerned, it is not the quantity of time that is spent is counted, but it is the quality time with creative discussions spent would count.

Unwanted enthusiasm by junior executives only to gain the attention of top executives is bane of public sector. One junior level executive who used to ridicule marketing officers who are glued to computer as watching TV, used to call for morning meetings after he had finished his meeting with his top brass. Whatever he was loaded by his boss, he would transmit to his marketing team and demotivate them at the start of the day. He used to present himself always to be intelligent and busy and would be always showy. It was an organization already with less than 200 products in their kitty. On a fine morning this executive ordered his officials of marketing department that each marketing officer should give one new product each day. There were four marketing officers. Imagine each day 4 products and in a year for approximately 250 days nearly 1000 products would be suggested. Was it a worthwhile idea? Absolutely not. But his idea was to get at least one or two new ideas from the team and trumpet it to his top brass that he had found some new product. In that course of over- enthusiasm some good products suggested by some marketing official would be wrongly understood and a wrong product would come out.

A group customer wanted a smart card for swiping with an electronic chip in it and to be used as tap card. This idea was not supported by technology department. But for the sake of meeting out the request of the group a different product was suggested as a discount card. Such activity would have generated some expenditure. So originally what was suggested as revenue generating idea turned out to be an idea causing spending by management? The overriding importance given to some departments like technology department result in a situation where the profit earning product suggested by marketing team pales into insignificance resulting in a potential loss of revenue. Undue importance given to say technology department may end up in losing a profit earning product suggested by marketing team thereby resulting in a potential loss of revenue.

8

Identification of market

"Marketing department should define business tactics, norms for canvassing business, identification of market and synthesizing the market effectively for the benefit of the organization."

Identification of the market for bank products is the key strategy to be evolved by the marketing team. Targets which are to be achieved by bank as a whole is defined first. The general mistake happening in Indian Public sector banks is that the top brass would allot, rather, load the above responsibility on the heads of the regional or zonal executives, by simply arithmetically dividing the figure. Zones or regions would also divide these targets to branches falling under its jurisdiction. Eventually the branch manager would put the pressure on the branch staff more so on the officers who would have been already loaded with the office routines.

The BM or the officer concerned would take up the list of borrowers who had always obliged to bank at any call. Borrowers would be given the details of the product and would be virtually forced to take up the product, be it new deposits, combo loans, gold coin, insurance policy or credit card etc. This coercion would force the branch staff to identify again and again the same customers to push the products. This approach would only drive the customer away from the bank instead of staying with the bank. The selection of the party would be either deposit or advance customer.

Instead of giving a line command that the total target should be vertically divided by the all branches, marketing department should be assigned the task of fixing targets depending up on the potential of the branch. The marketing department should also evolve a suitable strategy for pushing the product based on the vertical marketing or horizontal marketing techniques. What is the use of sending large number of gold coins to a rural or small branch where there may not be sufficient customers for taking the gold coins? Similarly dumping insurance products to rural branches would only make the local branch manager dump these products on the gullible innocent villagers who may not understand the meaning and implication of such insurance products. The result will be dangerous. The incoming manager might find it very difficult to survive in that branch for quite some time. There is also a possibility the villagers may become angry and damage the reputation of the branch and bank and also personally put the branch staff to jeopardy.

Marketing department should analyze the product first and then identify the potential buyer be it an individual, institutional or industrial buyers of their product. It should then engage in the process of creating market through marketing activities like campaign, stall activity in both vertical and horizontal planes. After identifying the possible users of the product, marketing department should put the product across the branch managers first for them to know what the product is and to get a feedback whether the product would find takers in their local area. After identifying the potential for the product, targets can be fixed for the various zones or regions after getting it discussed with the heads for implementation.

Instead of putting the product to branch managers, marketing department can also take the suggestions from the branch managers for any new product. One such product is swiping machines. Many of the public sector banks' clientele require this swiping machine. Except one or two public sector banks, it is only the new generation banks or the private banks that has conquered the total market. Branches of the PSBs struggle with their corporate/head offices for issuance of swiping machines in vain. This is not only a revenue generating proposition, but it is a customer retention tool. Technology team quoting the lesser number of card usage, will decline to introduce this facility in the banking system. When they mean cards they should take it into account both ATM and Credit cards which is not generally done.

Another potential area for marketing lies in the government business. Generally some of the private banks are intelligent enough to take the lion's share of deposits of the scheme funds for their banks. The end users may not have account with them and they are also not bothered about it since they can always show the hand to public sector banks. Public sector banks would also start opening accounts imagining that a major chunk of funds would come to them without knowing that the funds had already been transferred to private banks. Public sector banks would be doing unprofitable job in serving the customers which involves a considerable cost without getting **the quid pro quo deposits** in to their bins. There is huge government business available for every bank depending upon their presence. The marketing department should plan strategy in such a way that the entire bulk of funds come to them first for which they do the proportionate service. In extending technology which is prevalent prominently in all these public sector banks, marketing department should evolve suitable plans for distribution of funds to the beneficiary which the state/central government identifies.

Even amongst the public sector banks there are certain banks which are intelligent enough to garner major share of big deposits for them and distribute the execution work to other banks, thanks to the net work arrangement with other banks. It is also seen that banks with more number of branches in a particular state, due to poor marketing strategy would lose the main deposit account and get to serve only due to compulsion. Unhealthy business practices result in a leveraged advantage to one PSB as against another which needs to be avoided by IBA or the regulator.

The CEOs of such public sector banks also play a major role in garnering business with some of them promptly covering the government departments periodically and taking the business. CEOs of some Banks may believe only in rapport with ulterior motive and remain a serving bank always without trying to garner the big business in wholesome manner.

Garnering big business falls under the responsibility of marketing department. Generally the branch manager gives clue about the potential business available. When the business is converted there is clash between the branch and marketing department in claiming the business. At times, the branch managers, thinking that the due credit may not come to them, will play a lacklustre role in follow up, leading even to a possible loss of business. This happens mainly due to lack of clarity of role between the department of marketing and the branch.

In many cases a business entity, an educational institution or government organization may open account in one centre and expect service from across branches in India. For example the branches may have to receive huge cash towards the main account, for which it will not have any benefit but rather some inconvenience would come because of excess cash holding. It may also result in collection of lots of data for the original account by the branch. Branch may not have sufficient manpower. Under such circumstances, the branch does not cooperate well as per expectation of the corporate/head office or the parent branch. This may ultimately end up in customer dissatisfaction.

Identification of market is useful for meeting out the temporary funds requirements of the banks. Banks have to meet their bucket positions and require funds temporarily to fill up the buckets. They will be approaching the same customers, may be some corporate or PSUs, who are potential bulk suppliers of deposits. The rate of interest plays a major role here. Institutions and corporate houses have financial analyst helping management in parking of sizeable funds for a short term. Knowing the urgency of the banks, they dictate terms for the banks on interest rates. In such a scenario the marketing team would be making all out efforts to bring those funds to their fold. At this juncture to put the marketing department in a fix, the branch manager will connive with the zone or region head and put the blame on the marketing department stating that the branch was preparing for paying interest on card rates and had canvassed the deposits, which were snatched by marketing department by paying higher rate of interest. Some junior executive cadre BM (AGM/DGM) would directly interact with CMD/CEO or ED and complain that the marketing department had foolishly acted. At times ZM/RM would reprimand the marketing department officials by directly calling them up, there by discouraging the entire marketing team. This may make the corporate not to extend the deposit which it had already committed and give it to some other bank which has better marketing strategy.

Thus marketing department should define business tactics, norms for canvassing business, identification of market and synthesizing the market effectively for the benefit of the organization. Conflict of interest between various departments should be definitely avoided. There should be clear cut norms for approaching the business sources so that maximum is mobilized. In fact the marketing department should take lead in formulating these things and impress upon the top executives about the modus operandi. The segmenting, planning for the business, fixing targets for the branches and zones/regions should be done in consultation with the marketing department. Any marketing activity initiated by the marketing department should be conducted promptly and properly to reach all the staff and instill in their minds that whatever they do will finally be recognized and rewarded.

At this juncture one should keep in mind the business operation of health industry. The cost of extending a patient's life for two days amounts to few thousand millions of dollars. Why doctors pay more attention to such patients. It is on one part improvement in scientific research and other part the principle of supply chain management. Behind the act of survival of the patient survives the hospital industry. What will happen if the patient dies two days before? Sure it may be critical in few cases but not in all cases. The big companies come forward to spend on corporate social responsibilities. How about the social responsibility of having brought the obesity and elderliness in the younger generation by supplying the margarine filled products and the carbonated drinks. It all comes under the principle of supply chain management. Identification of genuine market is an important assignment for marketing department.

9

Let someone else do it

"Whenever any extraordinary job needs to be handled, the marketing department has to raise up to expectation of the management and device a planning, marketing and implementation strategy."

Whenever any extraordinary job comes, the marketing department has to raise up to expectation and device a planning, marketing and implementation strategy. This is lacking in most of the public sector banks. When the junior level teams take up the job with all the enthusiasm, the top executive cadre hesitates to take up such new ventures. After the eruption of technology into banking services, mostly the experienced executives who are not well versed with technology hesitate to venture into new business. Many corporate houses want technology based services from public sector banks just because there is more accountability and cost benefit in using these services. Private sector banks generally extend these services as per requirements of the corporate but they charge sufficiently high so that the corporate tend to use these services restrictively.

In such cases when the corporate approach the public sector bank, the branch manager is unable to give a prompt reply to the customer and the customer contacts marketing department. When marketing department feels that the assignment can be taken up, instead of the needed support from the top level the attitude of "let someone else do it" creeps in. This has a dampening effect in the minds of the marketing officials.

Marketing Mantra "sell yourselves first before selling your product" applies more to these executives. Internal marketing is part and parcel of marketing methodology. When the Top Management Committee wants all managers and officers and clerks to sell themselves to other staff and customers as part of marketing technology, these executives who are decision makers should also think of applying this to themselves.

The chapter heading "let someone else do it" is a razor edge. In an organization the management may want to gift some reward to performers. The bank may have gift card in its shelf. Instead of using the gift card which is hassle free for the bank, if the bank wants to gift the performers with some gift coupon from some other corporate with restrictions attached to it on usage so that the gift coupons are used to the extent of 10 or 20% only by way of redemption or purchase, then the scheme becomes a total flop since the receivers of such coupons may not be able to encash them in time. This not only denies the employees their incentive but also results in a loss to the bank as the coupon issuing companies may not take back the unused coupons. The marketing department would have been the right choice to implement the scheme.

"Let someone else do it" does not fit in well in credit card business. In credit card, communication is the key factor for bringing in customers as well as retaining them. Most of the private sector banks indulge in excellent communication with the credit card customers. Any new update should reach them in time. When a customer remits his dues it should be reflected immediately at the earliest. When private sector banks communicate about any NEFT/RTGS remittances within an hour or at the latest by a day, Public sector banks take two or three days for acknowledging the receipt. Similarly when the customer is in dire necessity say he is held up in a restaurant since the card is not working he would expect immediate help from the bank which has issued the card. There should be spontaneity in attending to such calls. Some of the public sector banks never take this aspect seriously. The credit card in charge be it any level, Chief Manager or AGM would extend the formula "What I can do for that" or let someone else sitting in Call Centre or service provider's office attend to it. They may even threaten these call centers or service providers not to divert such calls to them. Ironically such person's name would be available in the website of the bank for contact. When a customer in distress does not get any relief by reaching the contact numbers what is the use in calling such contact numbers?

10

Dearth of service in third party products leaves a bad impression

"When marketing department takes up an assignment and proceeds with marketing strategies, the top level should ensure that the concept is well received and there are no mistakes in the concept."

What are third party products? Any service/product not directly offered by the bank, but being a product of some other financial agency is called third party products. Examples are life and non life insurance, medical insurance, mutual funds, gold coins and even credit cards marketed by banks.

When the bank sells such products to its select customers, even though the bank is doing as a corporate agency or a channel partner, the customer gets an impression that it is being done by the bank itself. So the bank has to be doubly careful in serving such clients. The general tendency amongst PSBs is that the bank officials show some interest in these products at the time of selling them to the customers. But while serving the customers they do not evince the same interest. In certain cases like unit linked insurance policies the customer has to be briefed first, educated about the investment in market securities. The different varieties of investment patterns should be taught to him if he does not already know about it. The customer should be advised to change over to various options depending upon the market activities.

Without doing these preliminary things many of the Banks had taken premiums from the customers. Many customers, unable to renew the annual premiums, discontinued the policies. The result was that they not only heavily lost their premium already paid after adjustments of charges by the insurance companies but also the confidence level with the banks. Similarly many mutual funds would perform well depending up on the market condition only. The right time to come out of the scheme should be properly advised by the bank. Many private sector banks had dedicated team of officers to attend to this. But the disadvantage with the PSBs was the lack of such team and many a good customer had a bad experience with the bank.

When marketing department takes up an assignment and proceeds with marketing strategies, the top level should ensure that the concept is well received and there are no mistakes in the concept. For example, taking basic accidental insurance volitionally for all the customers has some hiccups and the customer may resist against the supposed minimum premium, to be deducted from his account. Not aligning with the market trend is a conceptual mistake. Credit card business for example is one area which only private sector and to some extent SBI have successfully handled. In credit card business, when every organization is giving points which can be exchanged for buying some items, some bank may think giving cash back to their customers for their earned reward points or waiving some joining fees, a better idea to draw lots of customers. After implementing this, top management would be questioning the marketing department that such good facility is not being brought to customer and marketing department is incapable of bringing business. It is unfortunate that the top management blames the marketing department, for lack of sales; though they are not engaged in the operational activity, leaving scot free the branch management which is responsible for distribution of credit cards. The banks should think what credit card base is there and what types of privileges can be given. Some customers would like to have excess charges levied by petrol bunks to be refunded by the credit card organization. Some may want their points to be collected over a period and used for redemption to buy a better good. It is very important to align with the market and extend such acceptable benefits so that you are neither blamed nor criticized. Similarly when some rewards are given by the management for its own staff for achieving some target they should involve in it and do it.

11

Tech Savvy – be a real one

"While introducing technology banks should ensure that they really make use of technology in very effective way."

Today all banking activities are based on technology. Every bank is using the technical platform to reach the customer. Being tech savvy is a source of competitive advantage to keep a bank in race. Banks while introducing technology shall ensure that they really make use of technology in a very effective way. After having accepted technology, no bank should go back and say that they have partially invoked technology. An occasion may arise when marketing department would have contacted a big business for issuing chip based cards in enormous numbers which would generate daily revenue. Or there might be a situation when a corporate may want funds transfer through prepaid cards in large number for their sales force throughout the country. Marketing department would be thinking that technology department would extend the correct technology for their requirement and would have positively apprised the customer that the service would be extended at the earliest. But in joint meetings they would be embarrassed to know that technology department is incapable of handling such requirements. It may not be really true that the bank lacks technology; it would be so, that the officials dealing such matter may not like to take up the venture since it would be an added burden on their department and even after the technical service is extended the credit would go to the marketing department. Hence Technology department would totally negate the idea of the product or service. This is a very painful syndrome prevailing in some PSBs.

Why this negation? When huge profit is sure in front of your eyes, all entrepreneurs do not grab the opportunity. Some hesitate to grab the opportunity thinking that whether they are really eligible for the same. This is a foolish situation. There are always some assignments in which price skimming takes place. Initially very huge profit would be booked followed by smaller profits by the companies. Just because the executive does not know how to do business he should not put the marketing department to jeopardy and mockery. Many executives of public sector doubt when such open opportunities are standing barely in front of them. They doubt that such opportunity is not certain and leave meekly the opportunity to a private sector bank. This is very much prevalent in banking sector. The correct approach will be that they are empowered to be technically superior and be really capable of supporting the marketing department on their technical requirements.

In PSBs every executive is mainly concerned about the addition of new customers and new business.

Not all the executives look into the factor **"Account Closed"**. This folder reflects the quality of customer service and marketing strategy. Every bank **should use technology** to analyze the accounts closed for every quarter. If the accounts closed reveal a smaller sum as balance in the accounts closed it is not going to be a worry. But if the balances in such closed accounts are huge and the reason for closing the accounts are not satisfactory then there is something else that has to be introspected. MIS department can effectively use technology to review closed accounts.

There are occasions wherein a bank might want to communicate to customers on certain issues. In today's scenario, the communication methods are numerous. Within few minutes lakhs of customers can be communicated. Here also technology plays a vital role. However every bank has some system and procedures. According to that a special permission might be required to be taken for using technology since it involves a cost. For example to inform customers about some incentives payable to them a mere SMS would be sufficient. But for that a special note might be required to be initiated. Instead of proceeding like that if the same is communicated through telephone over few weeks which do not require permission; imagine how much time it would consume for the department to convey the same to customers. What a futile attempt would it be? We need to be really tech savvy. Technology at the desk or at the finger tip is the new mantra of the younger generation to day. Imagine when most of the public sector banks are offering an android based mobile banking application, if your bank alone is not offering the same, the younger generation would rate you poor and technically incompetent. Marketing department markets any product with confidence expecting a service level support from the technology department. Another example to mention here is viewing of credit card statement. A link to view the credit card statement when clicked, if it shows a message that the link is not a dependable one and there may be security issues in proceeding with that link, what will be the impression of the customers? It will be more intriguing if the caution is exemplified by showing "http" instead of "https" in red with a crossing over it. This type of links with warning messages will give technology department, why for bank itself, a joker image. Educated and tech savvy customers would laugh at it.

12

Never be a launching pad always- also fly

"On many occasions it happens that the public sector banks happen to be training platforms for their young staff especially for those who seek a job in private sector with better emoluments"

Public sector banks have the habit of being launch pads only. They never try to fly. Rich experience is stuffed in Public Sector Banks' staff. Any new person is developed by a public sector bank, nourished till such time he grows to give yield. When the yield starts, these banks simply leave the person to a private sector bank by meekly surrendering. They lose the potential of earning rich dividend. It is like educating a child and abandoning him when he starts earning. Most of the public sector banks are addicted to this habit of abandoning. It happens with new products too.

It should be known that in Tamil Nadu, the services of ATM were started by a Chennai based bank as a pioneer and this was followed on by others. Having started such wide network, whether the advantages of it were ploughed back? This might be a valid question. Similarly introducing core banking solution was also pioneered by a south head quartered bank. Whether this technological advantage was really fully made use of?

Why such doubt should come to the mind? It is because, after having launched such excellent services, the quality and profitability or business volume had not galloped to the extent it would have been expected. This reflects a sorrowful state of lack of communication between different levels of management and lack of sustainable marketing efforts.

Public sector banks should not only be a launching pad but they should also try to fly. Public sector has a huge potential and is a knowledge reservoir. In fact, they have been setting systems and procedures for many activities in banking. These banks should not only encash on such experience but also sustain that earning potential without leaving the opportunity to private sector bank. This does not mean that they should spoil the private sector bank's earning potential. When they have grown up a child, it is but natural to make the child work for their family.

Why the effort stops with launching only, but not used for enhancing the potential earning? It is because the junior level executives, who are supposed to be the performers or executors in the triangle of organization, wish to align with the top most executives only and not with reality. These executives wish to satisfy their top brass and be in good books of their top brass. They hesitate to share the real crux of the issues at many stages and fail to discuss with the top brass about the new product or initiative simply because they feel that the top brass may not like the idea or may not understand that idea.

On many occasions it happens that the public sector banks happen to be training platforms for their young staff especially for those who seek a job in private sector with better emoluments. These public sector banks make the cow or child grow and hand it over to private sector when it starts fruition.

13

Unlearning and paradigm shift

"The paradigm shift from service orientation to profitability is the need of the hour to make the bank activities more profitable. Profit orientation should be the prime mover while looking for a paradigm shift without compromising the customer service or government guidelines."

Any organization should believe in change and position itself to handle such a change to achieve new developments.

Unlearning from your mistakes and myths is yet another negative paradigm shift. Public sector fails to make the required paradigm shift at the right moment and that is why many of the attempts of public sector have ended in as a low result venture.

A butter bee starts flying when it comes to top layer of water in pond. From that time onwards it never turns back on the path it has come. It starts aiming at new things and new ways of life. Similarly public sector even though is formed to serve the public at

MARKETING, THE SACROSANCT MANTRA

large, should aim at going with new traditions and new avenues and should not linger on to the old system of serving only the poor alone. It does not mean they should shun away the poor. There are certain schemes in which they volunteer to encourage the poor. But in today's environment the gen Y does not want a crowded branch where in they cannot get their jobs done on time. Similarly a corporate does not want to engage in potential danger of dealing in such crowded environment. So what should be the strategy of the bank? When a bank boasts itself a technically superior entity, it should pass on the technical advantage to the younger generation and the corporate. They should device a system by which they specially handle both the types of customer. There are potentially two classes of service. One service is for the poor and needy which does not generate higher profit margins. Another service is service to the HNIs and corporate which generates copious returns. The bank should have such paradigm shift in its philosophy of customer service that balances both sectors and the bank rises up to the expectation among the public and also generates sizable revenue.

Top management in banks should believe in the art of unlearning and paradigm shift to move towards profitability management without compromising on quality of service. For the sake of satisfying some higher officials, be it Central Bank's executive or MOF official, the CEO of the bank should not accept unviable proposals. He should balance nicely such that proposals which are not profitable are sidelined and proposals which would generate revenue are grabbed at the earliest. The bank would have gone through various experiences on different projects. From those projects and proposals these public sector banks should unlearn lots of non value adding activities and encourage a paradigm shift in thinking so that there is double side effect on growth.

Brand visibility and re branding are part of unlearning and paradigm shift. Why some corporate give more importance for the brand visibility and reach. Why some big banks especially in the private sector go for rebranding by spending a sizable amount. When there is a paradigm shift on the values of the organization it should reach the customers who exist and it should also attract the new customers into its fold. It can also be considered as yet another P in marketing. It is Called Physical Evidence. The Bank logo which is attractive, the catchy sentences, the vision or mission statements all form part and parcel of physical evidence.

Many public sector banks, hesitate to do this rebranding in the right way possible. Brand visibility is one factor which is very important in today's banking parlance. Many banks, of course are expected to take financial inclusion in a committed way, go in for normal products and services for the sake of showing higher ups that they have done as per directions. Similarly showing more than the expected percentage of specified business, say priority sector lending more than 40 % does not mean a better rating would be given. It is that factor which would glorify the bank that meets out the requirement of all stake holders. In other words a bank should not only meet the central bank's requirement but also meet the requirement of the stake holders. The paradigm shift should be to make the bank more profitable one and profit orientation should be the prime paradigm shift without diluting the customer service or government guidelines.

14

Concept delay and Concept dying

"Financial inclusion product has to come from Rural Banking or development or branch expansion cell, because they only know about the requirement."

Various new business concepts surface unexpectedly in public sector only. By the time the concept is developed and brought out as business decision the concept is lost. The delay in enacting the concept or delaying it so much that it is tantamount to concept dying thereby exposing the public sector to a great loss.

When banks were given flexible options to charge interest on loans especially on home loans, some banks ventured first thereby attracting takeover from private sector banks. The private sector was rattled at that time and it was learnt at that time, the matter was taken up at apex level too for discussion. The banks which quickly reacted to the situation made good business. There were similar occasions in which any concept which was introduced without delay had always earned benefits.

Call Centre, Digital display media, Face Book and twitter are some of the concepts which are either delayed or made to die in public sector. When the private sector banks have started using the same in very effective manner, many of the public sector banks are still struggling to introduce the concept weighing the pros and cons of implementing such concepts.

Undoubtedly public sector has got more accountability and responsibility towards such concepts. They should go through the concepts and implement whatever is possible thereby making the concept not to die or get delayed.

While implementing such new concepts like call centre or digital media each public sector bank may have some vision and forethought in implementing the scheme as per requirement of their bank. Generally such implementation processes are copied from one public sector bank or other and similar model is envisaged. While doing so the originality is lost. The other bank would have some idea in their mind in establishing a call centre or digital display media. Without understanding their inner idea and requirements some other public sector banks copy the process or methodology with the result that the concept is lost or it dies. Similarly the concept level delay equally ends in non delivery.

When there is concept delay or there is a situation that the concept is lost due to time delay, the mid-level executives should impress upon the top management to find suitable solutions for it as they wield administrative power. The middle management namely CM/AGM are the executing authorities of the plans of Top management team. Hence it is the duty of these middle level executives to impress upon top management to avoid concept delays and make the concept alive and implement it in shortest time possible.

The CEO/CMD may have some itinerary in his mind as per his requirement. It may be some APEX level Bank officials visit, or ministry of finance officials visit or Central Bank's official visit. When he has concern that event should pass on smoothly he does not mean other errands are to be kept in abeyance. He would never say to keep other things pending and do that activity alone. However he would reiterate that his priorities are very important and hence it should be attended to in a professional way. Taking clue from this the junior executives put all other papers into rest and attend to this main programme of CMD/CEO so that the event passes off nicely. After making a review only the pending matters are taken up for action. By that time if any other requirement comes from CMD/CEO then again the matters are put on hold and CMD/CEO's work is attended to. This involves a total concept delay or it makes the concept to die by itself.

The transition stage from CM to AGM plays a crucial role in this concept delay. A person as a chief manager would have given importance to the concept, based on the input of the junior officials. But once he becomes an AGM, there is a paradigm shift in his policies and viewing things. He thinks that meeting out the requirements of top management alone is his first priority. Every day whatever the top executive has in his mind, becomes the priority of the junior level executive, namely AGM or CM. He is not worried about the pending proposals that are to be attended to so that zones or branches would be executing their business in time. He prefers to keep them in pending lest the Top executive's work is delayed.

Another reason for the concept delay is that the original department from where the product has to emanate does not float the product. For example, a call centre installation or digital display media should be taken care of by technology department. Similarly any rural banking oriented product should emanate from Rural Banking department. Financial inclusion product has to come from Rural Banking or development or branch expansion cell, because they only know about the requirement. If any one of these involved departments orders any other department to bring such product, there will be only confusion. It will be more embarrassing to see that one department authoritatively dictates another department for doing an activity.

A public sector bank may recruit directly from good universities on Campus Mode, MBAs with marketing as specialization to work for marketing department. But before recruiting them there should be an analysis of the concept, "how are we going to use these MBAs" There should be coordination between the HRM department, marketing department and the Top level Management Committee who had taken this decision. Having recruited them, it may be necessary to give them on the job training for knowing the products or its applicability. While undergoing the training itself their tenure for training should be crisply defined and implemented. In present day scenario all public sector banks are losing bunch of employees going out of banks due to retirement. Under such conditions the local branch manager would not like to leave the employees posted to his branch even if he is a marketing manager. The branch manager would like to retain him at any cost because it will take more time to train one such person again. All such requirements will push the branch manager to approach the zonal manager to retain these marketing officers for their branch. If the zonal managers impress upon the chief executive to allot these people for the branch then the original concept gets delayed or dies. Marketing department if at all it has prepared some plans keeping these marketing men in mind will lose their plan. HRM department has to again recruit people for marketing department if there should exist one. Thus concept delay or concept dying is so prevalent in public sector that meaning of "marketing" is always lost. Many a time the marketing team is mired in conflicting directives to do non qualitative jobs that tantamount to non value adding activities.

15

Which is correct approach? Dogmatic or pragmatic

"Every batch of marketing officers will be imagining a position of doing something creatively, but seeing the scenario existing in the bank they would decide to associate themselves with the branch activities than marketing activities."

In the case of officers of marketing department being used for other purpose by the Zones, When the CEO of a bank submits himself to the pressure of zones; the approach to marketing is vitiated. To be dogmatic, the CEO has to retain the officials to marketing department which is the correct approach. In a pragmatic approach he may accede to the request of zonal managers and use them as officers at the branch. Then, for the bank and for the marketing department, this is not a healthy approach. Every batch of marketing officers will be imagining a position of doing something creatively, but seeing the scenario existing in the bank they will decide to associate themselves with the branch activities than marketing activities. Unless there is some force which restrains this idea and retains the officials to marketing department, the recruited marketing officials also may not stay with the organization, if they believe in marketing as their real career. Temporarily it may suit some people but a person with lofty goals to have a successful career in marketing will not stay with the organization. By then, any realization by the bank management will be too late. After all, late repentance will never be true and true repentance will never be late.

Marketing activity will go a waste if it is tagged on to the branch. The dogmatic approach or the pragmatic approach of the branch (or branch manager) would tell the performance on the business. Marketing officers allotted to a particular branch will also struggle due to the attitude of the branch manager. In many public sector banks there had been lull period when the top executive might be constrained to take liberal loan sanctions. Any third party product selling, as for as public sector banks are concerned, has a direct bearing on this whether any bank accepts or not. Even though the regulators put lots of restrictions in discouraging dumping third party products to the loan or advance customers, the reality is different. Many borrowers do oblige the branch managers.

During such periods of low activity by the bank on the whole, the top executives, zonal managers may not be able to take decisions on big proposals. There will be hesitation on the part of management to do so. Any superior passes the ball to the junior most one possible and escapes unhurt. The gullible juniors if they are not intelligent enough will face severe action for the wrong doings from the same old boss who has passed on the ball. "Once bitten twice shy" attitude will develop amongst the lower cadre also and they will stop sanctions. In such situations no top level executive gives comfort level to their subordinates. However there are definitely certain exceptions among them. One of the south India based banks rose up again because of the CMD who gave comfort level to all the officials and instilled confidence in them. Senior executives should instill confidence in the minds of the field level people. Because managers are constrained to perform, the targets of the marketing officers would not be reached. Marketing officers will be finding potential customers but managers will not be meeting out their requirements. The requirements of such customers would depend on the Manager's sanction.

When a marketing manager is given target, there should be a dogmatic approach of bringing say 100 eligible - repeat eligible customers to the branch or manager's desk. From then on it is the responsibility of the branch manager for converting the contacts into business. When the marketing officer does not have rights or power to sanction a product be it a loan or service, then where is the question of fixing specific target for him? There should be a balanced dogmatic and pragmatic approach while defining the role of the marketing manager.

I had contacts with many marketing officers of other banks. Everyone would give an interesting experience. Our sharing of these stories was not to demean anyone but to understand the situation and act accordingly.

There was an event of an executive calling the meeting of all marketing officers for tuning up performance. He had come from different organization wherein lots of qualified marketing professional had been recruited. He thought that the new bank will also have such professionals. In the meeting he wanted to show his caliber. Generally the top executives mention about their son or daughter as an example more so if they have finished MBA. They would be saying that they were continuously learning from their wards.

When the head count was done he was annoyed that there were very few professionals with MBA qualification. Also when deep conversation took place, he came to know that all the marketing officers were used as mere servants by many zonal/regional offices. Unable to continue his conversation, he had said that he would consult his top boss and revert back to them. The fact was he never turned up for meeting those officers again.

Another experience was about a Keralite Executive who said that marketing officers are like Trichur Elephants and their duty was to get well dressed and stand as elephants of Trichur pooram festival. Probably that was a pragmatic approach?

One more event was about preparing request for proposal by one bank for a particular project. The department junior officers had prepared with great care the required clauses and submitted it to the junior executive. The junior executive went through the proposal, called the officers and handed over the documents of another bank and asked him to minimally change and submit. The original work done by the officers went unnoticed and the junior executive made just some alterations and submitted to his top brass which was immediately approved. The service provider had told the junior officers at a later period that the document was just a copy of another bank. How to categorize the act of that junior executive? Was it to be regarded as pragmatic approach?

A senior manager who was a professionally qualified person gave a different story. He had to answer all top executives in addition to his marketing executive. Like a police station where few policemen would be thrashing the culprit, all executives would chide him and his executive and mock at. Other department's executives would ask him whenever they met him, "Is there anything really taking place in Marketing?", "Acha! You do something in marketing department?" and "What is happening in Marketing Department?" He used to manage so nicely that he would deviate from the topic and come out without scathing. Somehow he would catch up the attention of the top executive at crucial meeting and prevail over with his ideas.

The story of another senior manager was very interesting. His Marketing Department was asked by personnel department to prepare a plan for making use of 300 and odd marketing officers who would be soon recruited. He was asked to prepare a training and deployment plan. He made a detailed plan by allotting the officers to various branches across India and segregating them as per requirements. He had made a detailed training plan and follow up for the same. After few days he was eagerly waiting for instructions from his immediate (junior executive) boss for further move. To his disappointment, he came to know that all the marketing officers had been asked to join branches since there was heavy pressure for staff requirement. To his disappointment later when he had gone to one of the branches, he could see those marketing officers doing pass book printing work and handling "May I Help U" counters. This was called as "Learning the Work" by the top brass of his organization. Thereafter neither he nor his junior executive opened up their mind. They obliged simply what their superiors instructed.

Pragmatic or dogmatic approach, it is the concern for the customer and his requirements which should dominate the thought process of bank managements.

16

Marketing is all Pervasive across the Pyramid

"The selection of personnel for marketing department should be made carefully. The staff should be dedicated, creative, imaginative, informative, inquisitive, innovative, intelligent and industrious."

It is said, higher executives in ruthless power or in number one position in any organization talk at times non sense. They escape since there is no higher official above them to take action. The same executives when switch over to other organizations at national level get easily trapped and some even lose their portfolios or get demoted. There may be jokers, critics and dedicated masters too. It has been felt very much because of these dedicated masters' quality only; organizations had escaped from the hands of these jokers or critics.

It is not uncommon to see in PSUs that executives try to highlight their roles always. They ignore to praise the exemplary service provided by their department or colleagues. They blame weaker departments and draw the attention of top executives towards their own personal achievements.

In the pyramid structure of organization, the CEO holds a prominent position. He should display his marketing skills and allow the same to permeate down to the bottom of the pyramid. It is like homogenization principle. When cyanide is taken, death takes place immediate only because of this homogenization principle. The top brass should depict the quality of marketing and then only down the line other executives would try to inculcate that marketing man's quality. In a line type of PSB, the CEO/CMD's views percolate through ED/CGM/ /GM/AGM/CM. Hence, the CEO is very much responsible in expressing himself. He should be careful not to leave a negative message to his subordinate. A CEO should understand the difference between marketing and selling. He should understand the role of marketing and give desired privileges and provisions so that the marketing department is able to implement the schemes. He should always consider that marketing is a vital department and deserves the top most attention. He should develop dedicated staff that can conduct surveys, get feedback on products and services, conduct campaigns, road shows and above all should leave the brand image of the bank in the minds of the customers and bring customers into bank's fold which in turn brings business to bank.

"Bullet point habit" is sarcastic joke floating around public sector bank. Some Top Executives have the habit of putting everything in bullet point for easy understanding. They may not be able to grasp the whole paper in one stroke. To make it easy, the lower executive will be putting the points in bullet point pattern. It is like index in a research reporting. But it has limitation. As a marketing initiative, one of the junior executive may try this concept in a rotating hoarding on the main road of a city wherein the by passers note the display. Imagine if the junior executive is so obedient to execute his master's bullet point idea that he puts all product details in a bullet point model. How many seconds the passerby will devote to see this board. How much he would have grasped from the board?. The junior executive should have used his wisdom. This might attract nasty comments from many quarters since nothing will be readable or observable. In such cases the senior executive should have avoided the concept mistake at the initial stage itself and nipped it in the bud. Yes, marketing is all pervasive across the pyramid.

Another point where the CMD/CEO should mark an example is in the area of performance of marketing department. Performance in marketing is abstract in nature. No quantification can be done in marketing department's function. This fact should be perfectly understood by all the executives in the organization and all the departments should try to effectively use the services of the marketing department for their advantage so that effective usage of marketing department emanates. One top level executive used to acknowledge with chocolates, whenever marketing department reported an achievement.

If the top management is more concerned about the target vis a vis performance, then it should create a sales department and marketing department could guide the sales department in reaching the target. Marketing department should operate on 24x7 basis. The selection of personnel for marketing department should be driven by the requirements of corporate policy on marketing. The staff recruited should be dedicated, creative, imaginative, informative, inquisitive, innovative, intelligent and industrious.

Marketing department should not be made a scapegoat or used as a cushioning department by any other department. No other department should be allowed to talk ill of the department and the CMD/CEO should keep the prestige of the marketing department high. Any executive of any department speaking ill of marketing department should have a feeling that he is speaking ill of the CMD/CEO. Such should be the importance for the marketing department.

The Chief Executive of the bank should know how to blend the fraternal departments to marketing department. The main departments that are complimentary to the marketing department are planning, development, corporate communication, public relations and retail loans department. The blend should be in such a way that the target actions of the marketing departments are reached nicely.

One peculiarity with the senior executives of the public sector banks is their aversion to spend for marketing activities. If the marketing Department comes with a request for some advertisement, say in the case of a south based bank, for releasing an ad to be released in south they will say why in south when all the people are well aware of the bank. If the expenditure is for north, they will say why north, anyhow no one will know our bank in north, then why such huge expenditure.

It should be understood that even well established brands go for rebranding in the market at phased intervals, to sustain their market share if not penetrate into others.

The foremost factor any senior executive of the marketing department should understand is identification of the product and the customer. The functioning of the marketing department will add value only when this classification is done. It is the big question like "EGG or CHICK FIRST". The Bank should decide whether a product will be prepared to suit the specific needs of the customers or customers will be identified for the specific product.

For eg a current account with fixed deposit facility is to reach customers who can specifically use such a product. Then it becomes customer specific. Vertical marketing technique should be used in such case.

Similarly any third party product should meet out the requirement of the customer and it will be generic. For eg gold coin, should be sold with the help of horizontal marketing technique.

In both these cases the marketing department should device the marketing strategy (method). The branch will be doing the selling and it will be called sales department. There is no question of fixing targets to the marketing department officials for these products. What is expected of the department is the technique with which the branch is expected to do the sale.

Marketing in general is like a tea shop especially a Keralite tea stall. When the tea shop is opened the owner will expect the customer to approach him. Once the shop survives for a month or so, then the tea shop owner will start reaching to the nearby offices by himself first and through his employees and occupy the entire area. The tea shop owner will be aggressively using both horizontal and vertical marketing techniques. This idea should be followed by the banks especially the public sector banks for which the marketing department alone can give the solution.

Many banks have tried to replace the old marketing official with management students from institutions of repute but the old aggressive marketing technique alone prevails.

To be precise, the survival instinct in a marketing official is the key for the survival of the bank and all efforts are needed to secure his position in the bank. After all, marketing is all pervasive across the pyramid.

17

Marketing and Technology are the interwoven twine of Banking

"Those officers, who had shown interest in TBC systems, were all considered for CBS eventually and no attempt was made to recruit sufficiently new people who were technically qualified to take up CBS seriously and effectively."

The above statement is a matter of fact.

When Banks changed from manual system to a computerized environment namely Total Branch Computerization promptly called as TBC, lots of officers got trained in that and comparatively but uniformly a sustained service was given to customers demanding lots of new and effective services. Many officers got well acquainted with such systems and they always enjoyed a special status. Normal transfer parameters applicable to other officers were not applicable for them. They were always called Xavier of the branches when their own branch novices were unable to clear any problem with the TBC system. After them, only the service provider would be the final authority and such service provider might have one or two who would stay continuously with such organization to attend the service calls.

Many such officers of PSBs would have become executives by the time Core Banking was put to use. With CBS in place many companies and many versions came up for application and it took sufficiently a sizable time to get settled with the software by each bank. Those officers, who had shown interest in TBC systems, were all considered for CBS eventually and no attempt was made to recruit sufficiently new people who were technically qualified to take up CBS seriously and effectively. Those who had rich experience in banking but less experience in technology or technical skills occupied very vital places in many banks. Of course good amount of training would have been given to these people to cope up the situations.

However it would have been better if technically qualified people had been trained in banking and then deployed in CBS so that technology and banking would have been seamlessly integrated. It would have facilitated the desired improvements in technology.

The real experience has been different. Many of the senior and middle management executives have knowledge in either banking or technology with the result there is always a sort of mismatch in understanding technical application to suit the customers' requirements.

As I said, there was always a message sharing between various bankers and such messages had always been very interesting and mind boggling but at times pathetic too. One such message was about clerks without even degree level education becoming an officer and getting into a vital seat in technology department. Since they were showing some sort of smartness over others they were retained in the department unduly and even junior and senior executives had to depend on them to a great extent. The guys would not reveal sufficient information to their superiors and their superiors would not also understand what they used to say even though they were technically qualified. It was learnt that good rapport with service providers made such people to exceed their powers as an officer and at times dictate on some products or services. Friends from that bank used to ridicule their management stating that if such persons were left out of the department then the normal functioning itself would be paralyzed since they had kept all the clues to themselves. Similarly there were many officers who were single handedly running hundreds of smaller programs and overstayed in Technology department creating an image that they were indispensable for the organization.

Why I should report the above thing? Not to be jealous of such people but because of the fact that these people simply discourage any marketing initiative to introduce new technology or new products. The marketing official would have brought out such a worthy contact which if properly had been implemented would have brought the bank a greater advantage. But these people would put barricade for such proposals due to ego or lethargy.

It was reported in the press that more than one public sector bank's ATM and net banking system collapsed for more than three or four days. These banks could not immediately bounce back to normalcy only because there might not have been sufficient technically skilled persons to clear the bugs. It was commented by many that non technical persons only had attended to such problems.

The idea is not to demean the effort of any non technical person but the idea is to rationally use real technical team to take care of technology department. It is desirable that the technology department is headed by a technically qualified youngster who can draw out the type of interface needed between technology department and other banking activities.

Many Bank managements had been categorically stating that they wanted youngsters that too the right person for the right job. But when it came to the consideration of executive post for technology department they had promoted mostly non technical executives to such position. This has definitely jeopardized the interest of organizations.

There was another case of letting down the marketing teams' effort. There was a multi transport system coming to metro cities. When the MTS wanted the banks to come forward for technology oriented service, banks headquartered in the same place did not come forward to take up such opportunity as they were not confident of taking such a responsibility. Knowing this a foreign bank had contacted the public sector bank to extend such services as back end since they did not meet out the RFP requirement with regard to their presence. It was also reliably learnt that the offer was declined quoting various reasons by most of the PSBs. Even though many PSBs had attended the briefing sessions, few had the capability to take up the assignment, none came forward to take up the service immediately – lack of confidence. Either the giant bank or any new generation bank would clinch that offer which would be revenue generating, technology oriented, making grand visibility and more particularly reaching the younger generation customers

The above event demonstrates how a revenue earning potential identified by the marketing team is allowed to let go due to the lack of confidence that has betrayed the technology department. It could have been due to the reason that a person who had been well versed with both technology and banking would not have been at the helm of affairs.

Again I will take further steps to explain the heading. On any product a marketing team would analyze the plus and minus and offer the product to the customer. The customer would be convinced by the marketing official about the product. When the customer wants to go with the product or service he would expect the same features as put forth by the marketing man. When he faces some hurdle then he would immediately take the marketing team to task and not technology group. A cohesive team of marketing and technology would be fine to address many issues raised by the customers and thereby enhance the business. That is why it is said that **Marketing and Technology are the interwoven twine of Banking.**

18

Team Building:
Who are members of the team?
Whether individuals or departments.
Who are the coordinators?

"A team has to be built on a strong foundation of good marketing principles. The team should have coordinators at various levels to effect transformation of marketing strategy into effective sales activity."

Before installing a marketing vertical, the prime job of any management is to build a team. The Team should be defined by the Top management who are the administrators. They should define the members of the team, whether individuals or departments. They should define the coordinators.

Marketing being a more abstract thing than selling should have a thread of connectivity. The nature of being abstract makes it a subject to be understood by each and every individual, so carefully, that at the end, implementation as required by top management is achieved. It is pertinent for effectively forming a marketing vertical; there should be not only a physical coordination, but a mental coordination between the members, departments in the whole organization. Why there should be stress for mental coordination? It is because for any sale of product to take place there should be a preceding marketing activity which is mentally coordinated.

Let us consider the business strategy of a popular garment maker. He will make an analysis of his product qualities, define his customers or potential area of support from public, make a strategic manufacturing activity, make sure of logistics necessary for distribution and finally go in for a marketing survey and locate the market. His marketing team would make the stock ready at the sale outlets.

Here comes the prime responsibility of the marketing team. It has to reach the customer's mind that there exists a product which will be of use for the customer. It has to impress the customer with the quality, price and comparability with the other products and make the buyer to take a decision to buy the product. It has to sufficiently attract the customer with possible discount, or freebies. It has to educate the depot or outlet salesmen on the salient features of the product and the USP to convince the customers to opt for this product. The customer might visit the Sales outlet quite number of times and ask for different questions. The salesmen should be trained in all these matters. The Salesmen should involve physically with imaginative explanations to the customer and capture the customer for the product. He should say the plus point of his product and the negative point of other products. That is why there would be some consumer durable companies who appoint their own salesmen in Sales outlet where multi brand products are sold.

It means that there should be a team, an effective team for any marketing activity. It should have coordination with various levels in the process of transferring the organization's goods to the hands of the customer. No team would come on its own and facilitate the organization for a joyful ride. A cross functional team has to be built on a strong foundation of good marketing principles. The team should have coordinators at various levels to effect transformation of marketing strategy into effective sales activity. There should be an integrated activity right from making the product available at the outlet to the point of trans-placing the product into the hand of end customer.

Team Work concept: capturing power in politics, how?

There were issues unattended by many political parties. Pan India corruption was deep routed. Any straight forward person entering police force, administrative force, railways, Electricity board, direct or indirect tax office had to bend their ways for survival. Amongst such forces few individuals made their grit to survive and came together to fight corruption. Other leaders or parties were also fighting against corruption. But one group fought it in a planned manner. They defined the problem, identified the problem presented it to public properly and presented to public that they were capable of giving solutions to the problem.

Public had felt these problems as more intriguing and really they thought whether one could give solution. Many youngsters joined the group of protestors and supported them. The team marketed themselves with capability. They impressed the public that they had the solution in their hand by conducting themselves. This was nothing but internal marketing. When the public felt that they would be capable of giving a solution and when a chance was given, these people presented themselves remarkably and won the elections.

In marketing parlance it is a must to have an integrated activity for any political party to sell their party to the minds of the public. People had the votes as coins or notes and the party had the political ability as their product. The product got exchanged for the coin/note like money with the product namely the political ability of the winning party.

The main idea of giving this example was not to exemplify any party in particular. But in pan India there was a feeling that no government without adjustments or corruption in their team could survive. The party made known to public that they could give good governance by following simple means of execution.

19

Then what sales really is?

"It is the triggering of a program, firing of a cracker; it is countdown of space craft."

Marketing activity is like making a computer program for application and sales activity is triggering such program; Marketing activity is like making a cracker and sales activity is igniting or firing of such crackers; Marketing activity is like readying a space craft and Sale activity is setting the countdown activity. Making the various products to the branches and branch staff and making it visible to the customer is the activity of Marketing. Firing the idea into the customer to buy the product, triggering the idea in the minds of the customer to go in for your bank's product, starting the countdown in customer to decide your bank's product are all sales activity. Having many products and making the field level functionaries like front line staff, Branch Manager, Zonal/Regional managers to know the product is the success of marketing department. Any amount of product availability, product quality, any better pricing of your bank's product would not be sufficient to catch hold of a customer if the field level functionaries like desk clerk/officer, Branch Manager, Regional/Zonal manager do not know what your products are. A successful desk staff gets the needed product inputs to push the product from the marketing team. A successful branch in charge gets the relevant strategy to push the product from the marketing team. Nonetheless it is the duty of the marketing team to communicate the required product and customer information that might be required by the sales team at the prompt time. Any management which understands this subtle difference between sales and marketing only will do wonders for bank. Without understanding the nuances of marketing and sales, more so understanding it wrongly, no individual in a bank can think of becoming a manager/zonal manager or top executive of the bank.

20

Marketing strategy does not differentiate between people, cadre or hierarchy

"When it is a strategy, it is the whip from the high command. It is just like ringing the bell for any show. The organizer only decides the time, but the bell is rung by a peon only."

In a public sector bank, Gold coin department adopted a marketing strategy. Generally Branches would be advised to hold coins as per branch requirement. The reason was that the branches should not overstock gold and blink on a later date to find takers. This was a strategy for the bank as a whole. It might be noticed that many branches headed by AGM/DGM would be holding hundreds of 1 gms gold coin. Very few branches under scale 1 or 2 (ie smaller branches) would be holding few 1 gm coins and one scale I branch manager might be holding just one 1 gm coin. Central office/HO AGM/DGM would pounce on that poor branch manager who is holding just one coin, but would keep mum with the DGM of the branch who is holding hundreds of coins. Why such attitude. Because on a later date if the same AGM/DGM who is now branch manager becomes administrative head or his superior, then the official who is following up gold coin sale would be in jeopardy. Corporate office while shooting letter to branch manager holding one coin, may not send similar letter to a branch headed by an AGM holding more gold coins. This is an unhealthy discrimination.

In certain cases a branch might arrange for engaging of a service provider without taking the proper permission from HO. It might be a DGM headed branch. For availing such service, any nationalized Bank would have some system for approval. The department at HO would expect any branch to approach them seeking for providing such services through them with a proper approval from the higher executives. Similarly for approving any service free of charge, Banking operations department or any other suitable department has to permit the branch for going ahead with such activity. The branch would be expected to give cost and benefit analysis for such activity and based on net profit possibility the activity will be taken for charge free operation. In the above mentioned cases the DGM head of the branch might have taken certain assignments for free of charge and also engaged a service provider for a higher rate than the approved one and also a different service provider than the one suggested by the corporate/head office. On getting the information, the junior officer in the cadre of Chief Manager/AGM in corporate/head office would keep mum since he was afraid of facing the DGM. A parallel activity if done by a smaller branch manager in the cadre of Scale I where in the same chief manager/AGM might take the branch-in- charge to task instead of guiding him on the future course of activity.

The authority to approve any activity by a branch rests with the head office or corporate office of any bank. It is to be noted that the official exercising that authority may be in junior management cadre or middle management cadre or top management cadre. That is immaterial. For the branch he sounds like the highest authority of head office or corporate office. The executing official might be junior in rank to the official of the branch. It does not mean that the high cadre branch official should disobey the order of the junior executing official of corporate office or head office. When it is a strategy, it is the whip from the top high command. It is just like ringing the bell for any show. The organizer only decides the time, but the bell is rung by a peon only. The peon is only an executor like the lower ranking official of corporate or head office. That is why the statement, "**Marketing strategy does not differentiate between people, cadre or hierarchy" should be meant in all real sense by any management.**

21

Subtle difference between Marketing and Corporate communication

"A matured corporate communication department would seek for marketing events, to enhance the image of the bank - be it a sports activity, an industrial activity or an exhibition at any educational Institution or big corporate office."

What is the mileage out of displaying a video presentation in the main city road displaying various products? What is it the bank gaining by spending on ads in the souvenir of big Institutes or holding international sports activities? What is the advantage of keeping special sign boards? Why do banks or for that matter various corporate maintain parks or traffic islands. It is the idea of Corporate Communication department and it is a way of communication itself. If one analyses the nature of work done by corporate communication department, he would understand that it is the primary part of marketing. When a Bank is opening a new branch, is installing a Call Centre or introducing a new Service or product, Corporate Communication prepares the advertisement for it and releases and makes known to public that the service or product is available at the nearest branch. It is a type of branding/rebranding. The department brings the impression and existence of the bank in the minds of the people. A matured corporate communication department would seek events, be it sports activity or industrial activity be it an exhibition at any educational Institution or big corporate office, to enhance the image of the bank. The way they take the mileage out of such activities marks their presence. Any good corporate communication activity would involve marketing team. It will be a prelude to marketing activity only. Only when there is good chemistry between corporate communication and marketing department the fruition will be better. There should be full coordination between these two departments. CCD is responsible for bringing out Calendars, Diaries, compliments, hand outs etc for distribution on behalf of the bank. It has to sit with the marketing department and make such materials as requested by marketing department so that the amount spent by the department is useful. The items like compliments, calendars and diaries give an opportunity to the branch manager, zonal manager or marketing executive/officer to talk to a client. That is an opportunity for them to bring in business. It is only a strategic marketing activity.

Imagine if the calendars are released by 15th of January, a hand out with holiday list reaches the customer after the month of March, a credit card cash back offer amount reaching the customer after 3 or 4 months, what would be impression in the mind of the customer?. How the coordination between these two departments is bonded, speaks about the strength of marketing department. Marketing Department should tie up with CCD or hold them in unison so that any activity by the CCD is fully utilized by the marketing department. A diary should reach the customer before the New Year begins. A hand out with calendar should reach the customer before New Year. Communication is vital for marketing department. If what is meant is not what is said then what it ought to be done remains undone. Corporate communication should communicate wholly about the bank, its products/services at all levels and it should be encashed by the marketing department promptly.

It is the practice of senior executives to expect gist of papers presented before them. There are many Bullet point executives pan India. One General Manager used to say that the word general manager means that he need not see matter in particular and he will see matters generally only. What he actually wanted to convey was that he is one person common for all and hence matters should be presented for decision making level only and not for discussion level. It means that the points should be given as gist in bullet points and based on those points the executive will take decision. Such executives when they head corporate communication department try to squeeze in maximum information within the pamphlet, ad material that the department produces. There are some executives who want bullet points in these brochures, ad materials without understanding the intricacy of it. The bullet points would deface the matter itself but still such of those people would want all points to come in one single page.

Corporate Communication department may hold some hoardings or moving digital displays in which the traveler by two wheeler or car may spend a small time like wink of an eye only. It may be few seconds and the ad or display should catch the eye of the traveler and then only the purpose will be solved. The Bullet point executive whether junior level or senior level would want all points in such displays, with the result, the total digital display of board itself would become waste. It is the duty of corporate communication department to take care of such executives and more so the duty of marketing departments to mend such junior or senior executives who play a dramatic crucial role in such bullet point displays. It is pathetic that some marketing executives seem to sincerely oblige their senior executives in implementing such ideas.

In most of the public sector banks Corporate Communications department only takes care of all public relations work like sanctioning advertisements, displays, maintenance of parks and traffic islands and other visibility measures in addition to holding press conferences, liaison meetings with government and corporate clients. All these activities are basically marketing in nature and marketing department should be taken into confidence and the top administering committee should keep this point in mind always and embed the department with marketing department for smoother functioning. The marketing department should also take mileage out of the activities of CCD and ensure that the customer is well reached by these activities and the branches will be poised for a better sales activity. Hence it is not wrong to say that between corporate communication department and marketing department there is subtle difference only.

22

What are third party products and their impact on marketing

"Stock Market operation is not popular with Indian public, especially with the public sector banks' customers. They believe the bank manager and in turn the bank manager believes the top brass."

There was a period earlier when the FDI was opened up, insurance players in private sector started to tie up with public sector banks for getting business. Government had also partially given its nod for such tie ups. What was the impact of such third party products? It was terrible and tremendous. Branch Managers were given target by twin bosses -their own and that of the insurance companies. It was reported by many in marketing field that executives from private insurance companies used to dictate terms to the officers of the public sector banks.

How was the business done?

No new party was brought inside the bank. Special team of officials selected for insurance business would go to branches, take the list of customers from the branch manager and take an appointment with him to explain the insurance product. They would sit on the head of BM and somehow tie up some insurance policy for the customer. Customer would also put up with the event since he would not want to displease the manager. He would pay off the amount of insurance premium from his current account or savings account and try to escape from the BM. After sometime, the marketing official would be given target for mutual fund schemes. Again the marketing executive would approach the branch manager, take the same list of clients and get an appointment to explain the products. Some customers would frown at the outset; some would still oblige and issue a cheque for at least some minimum amount. Some would use all tactics to evade these officials. After sometime these marketing officials would be given target for gold coins and the same process would follow. This time some may prefer to invest in gold and accept the product. The marketing official will also breathe easy. But the bane with public sector is; this process getting repeated for n number of times with the result the parties resent coming to the bank.

Behind the scene what is the impact? When the customer gives his cheque for insurance or mutual fund or gold coin his balance from his account gets reduced. The real effect is the savings account balance of the bank reduces or the core deposit of the bank gets reduced.

The convenient argument moved by the insurance companies was that the customer however would spend on such insurance/MF/Gold coins schemes and why he should spend it through some other bank. This argument coupled with other lots of consideration made the top managements to sell the arguments with tough branch managers who wanted to act patriotic to the organization. The damage is more when the customer issued his cheque from his current account because it was zero cost fund for the bank and hence more loss. Thus the customer's fund was transferred from either SB or CA to insurance company and from there to open market operation and back to insurance company with lesser or higher NAV and back to the bank's customer with higher or lower NAV. The overall impact as reported was a lower NAV only. Insurance companies also did not lose heart by this and they managed to reschedule the product or remodel the product and still reached the customer through some technique or other.

The saddest part of the story is when the customer comes to know about the loss he has sustained from such schemes because of non follow up or expert guidance from bank. The bank finally loses the customer to another bank more so to a private bank. Stock Market operation is not popular with Indian public especially with the public sector bank's customers. They believe the bank manager and in turn the bank manager believes the top brass. But ultimately both of them are let down when the market operation ends in a loss. Suddenly the Wealth Management team or development department team would also intervene and start giving new definitions and jargons which the customer cannot understand. In some public sector banks the wealth management team would proudly say that they would only give technical assistance and would not commit like some private/ foreign banks. Whatever be the case the third party products have totally let down most of the customers. The only exception to this might be quoted as gold coin sales in which because of the steep rise in prices many customers gained but not because of bank's guidance. It was also because of the savings habit of the customers.

23

"Play safe technique", the holy chant of Public Sector

"Most of the tech products, customer initiatives, call centre activities are all some of the activities, wherein one bank tries to follow up the other bank to play it safe."

When any new product or project is put up by marketing or any department for implementation, the immediate reaction of the executives is "play safe". Most of them would want to know whether someone else or some other bank has done or executed such things/ product/ project. Copy Cat mechanism or verbatim copy methods are immediately resorted to by many. The reason they would give is that all public sector banks are government's bank. They do not want innovation but want safe route. Lots of examples can be quoted. If one follows up the sites of south based banks or their intranet applications they would come to know of this. Most of the public sector banks' portals, ad materials, digital signages and annual result announcements would follow up some same sequence. Even the call centre activities of two of the public sector banks would be very similar. Similarly in automation also no continuity of sequence will be envisaged. In an automatic process like call centre activity, suddenly the technology department would try to introduce manual process. The ideal example is creation of T pin generation, ATM pin generation, SMS, balance enquiry. Some junior executive would suggest that in a call centre which is outsourced, bank's officers can verify some details sought by customers instead of giving them to service providers automatically and seamlessly. For thousands of calls with smaller durations is it sensible to verify manually for each customer's request? Why then a service provider? It would not be out of context to quote that almost all the public sector banks send their junior/senior officers to other banks for knowing the implementation methods before commencement. Tech products, customer initiatives, call centre activities are all some of the activities wherein one bank tries to follow up the other bank to play it safe.

As per the speech of a great Indian Saint, abundant information/products and services are available in nature. You channelize it to enjoy it. Some Brahmins offer prayers meticulously to Sun God at 6 AM, 12 Noon and 6 PM. There is scientific meaning in it. The half an hour time during such offerings see a special bio rhythm in man's body and the prayer utilizes the change for the good of the body. Elders have offered this as a prayer so that all will do that meticulously. Similarly the services that a customer would need should be studied by the public sector banks as per the requirement of the customers and they should offer such services to such customers so that they would start using it.

Another point the sages say is weight shedding. This is advocated by doctors also. All Human beings should maintain the required weight for the body. The Body Mass requirements are taught by professional gyms and studios. Our ancient sages have proved them through yoga and asanas. Weight shedding is good for the healthy body. In today's banking environment weight shedding or in other words product shedding is an important medicine for the healthy bank. The banks have to stay slim with a comfortable and simple product palette. Simplicity only reaches the customers. Already some of the public sector banks have more than 100 products in their palettes. This would confuse the customers. Mostly the intrinsic benefits of such products are also not transferred to the customers. For example a simple insurance benefit attached to the customer's SB account may not be intimated to him with the result in case of eventuality the customer's family may not use the benefit at all. There might not be any recording or registering of data for meticulous implementation. Why such queer action on some products or services by all public sector banks uniformly? Is it because government wanted to have healthy competition amongst banks? But from bank's angle, it is always playing it safe technique.

24

Cost determination, cost analysis and cost cutting are essential tools of Marketing

"Cost determination in the right perspective would also help in competitively pricing the product."

This may sound strange. Yes in fact the three tools are survival tools for the marketing department. A successful marketing department would wisely use these techniques for comparative pricing with various products and services offered by other banks. Any product or service requires in addition to land labor capital, involvement of the skilled man power, technology, distribution channels, hardware, software and telecommunication charges. How effectively all these elements are utilized speaks out the profit for the organization.

Cost determination is the process of determining the cost of each and every operation in enacting a service or product being distributed. The minutest expenses are to be identified and accounted for ascertaining the real cost of operation of service or cost of product. Cost determination will have relationship to non interest income and net interest margin of the bank. Effectively determining the cost also ensures selection or retention of products in the product palette. Cost determination in the right perspective would also help in competitively pricing the product. In today's environment, lots of public sector banks are clustered around a particular place, that there requires a clear difference in price of the Product/Service to be delivered. Each bank attracts the customer with lots of advertisements and marketing techniques. But the customer identifies that bank which gives "prompt service" at a better rate rather cheaper rate. The word "prompt" has a larger meaning than is meant.

Relevant cost for relevant product should be the mantra of PS banks. Rational tracing of cost to the product helps in product positioning strategies and the need to reduce cost to sustain the competitive edge in the business. It will not be out of place if the PS banks adopt activity based cost model in pricing and operational control of branch activities which are responsible to sell the bank products. It is time the PS banks used performance based incentives (not salary) for officers of the banks.

25

Understanding the customer and Differential pricing technique are also marketing tools

"The right marketing man will understand the customer's irrationalities correctly."

The USP of marketing person is his ability in knowing customer's mind. When the mind of the customer is understood, so is his necessity about the product or service. Once the product or service will fit in the requirement frame of the customer then most of the job is done. Differential pricing technique would set the customer to our product/service.

The marketing officer should understand what the customer is and what his requirement is. Then he plans for the same and presents it to the customer. The concept and vision of the customer and producer synchronizes and sales take place. This example is for not a single customer but all customers. To know the mind of the customers only the promotional methods and Advertisement strategies are used. An analysis of contemporary products is to be done for effective sales. In today's scenario all companies have come forward for free usage for minimum period or for concessional rates.

The right marketing executive will understand the customer's irrationalities correctly. What is the rationale behind using a particular type of detergent powder? If a video demonstration is arranged by genuinely using the same tinted clothes for washing using two different detergent powders, then both the detergent powders may lose their market because both will not be able to remove all the stains as is shown in their advertisement. But still why such huge amounts are poured on to advertisements? It is only to reach the minds of the customer and to create an impact in their mind that their product would meet out their requirements to some extent. Customer also knows that the product will not remove the dirt 100% but still believes that any one of the product does some justice. Which product impresses him is the capability of the marketing official and his strategy. I had opportunity to find a sales man inside a supermarket, repeatedly contacting routine customers showing his products and explaining its features. The salesman was thinking on any one day they would revert to his brand. He used to compare different products when the customers were entering the supermarket. On one such occasion the salesman intercepted a customer who was a known customer for MNC brand toothpaste and asked him whether he had chosen the same brand this time also. The customer replied negative. The salesman was happy. He then asked "then you have chosen my brand". 'No' came the reply. Curiously the salesman asked, "then which other brand you have chosen sir" The customer replied the brand. The salesman asked the reason for selecting the product. The customer gave a funny reply. The newly selected product was on offer. If two packets were purchased one more packet came as free. Any amount of convincing, any amount of image built by the MNC could not confirm the customer behavior correctly.

The customer makes an impact in his mind about any product in the following ways;

1. Performance wise how the product is
2. Deliverables expected from the product
3. Comfort level with the product.

The right marketing official evaluates the customer correctly. He continuously thinks what will make the customer happy. If the customer is made happy then he becomes your salesman. He becomes your marketing guy. Then, what will make the customer happy?

In banking parlance if you see any service extended or product sold should be usable without hindrance. The customer should have seamless service from the product. In other ways there should not be any requirement for the interference of any sort while using. After sales service should not mean that the product always requires service after sales. Some of the water purifier companies made a deep root in customer's mind because of this only. The same has also now changed and that is why lots of other companies have entered into this field.

A marketing man not only keeps the customer tagged to his product but also keeps the customer away from other products. How is this possible?

It is to be understood that every customer has a marketing person in his inner self. The inherent qualities of such customers should be understood and any product or service or the marketing concept should cater to this need and then only the customer will be attracted to the product.

Customer satisfaction and his value for money are two important factors that decide the customer's orientation. Product positioning strategies depends upon the customer's choice. Some believe in cost and some believe consciousness.

The customer does not stop with one product only. The finance super market should have all acceptable products in its kitty and a suitable product mix should be given to the customer. **Combo loan is one example.** When a customer goes in for a home loan he is given a car loan too. Thus the customer is given some interest benefit or processing charges concession. A differential pricing system pays dividend. Banks should apply different relationship pricing models by bundling products, by pricing products based on the behavior of customers, pricing based on the time limitation, pricing based on personalized behavior i.e higher price for customer based on his requirement and willingness to pay. Some of the foreign banks have come out with such products based on time based relationship, behavior based relationship, and loyalty based programs and value added packages.

The real marketing man would try to understand the customer behavior. He should well understand the issues related to the product and customer. Customer behavior issues concerning his product should be received recorded analyzed and rectified by the marketing man.

26

Product positioning is a strategy in banking parlance

"As a great sage would say, a car with 800cc capacity cannot think of formula one race."

"Similarly a customer knows to distinguish between a normal branded car and a Rolls Royce."

The banker should know thoroughly about his product first as explained above and equally his customer also. Why do people prefer to have a SB account or Current Account with a foreign bank than with a public sector bank more so a nationalized bank?

The foreign bank defines the product, service and defines the eligibility clearly. There is no ambiguity. Communication is very effective. They understand the requirement of the customer, customer behavior, their issues and solutions. They also do not extend the product to all. They define their customer as the customers decide their bank. Thus a product which suits the needs of elite customer is defined by the bank and presented to the select band of customers with elite customer service. These banks have common products as per stipulation of Central Bank, but there will be restrictions for the customers to have such products as he likes.

Thus the foreign banker Positions his product perfectly. He analyzes the customer well. Let us take the example of Maruti Cars. There are low end Alto 800 cars and high end Swift and Swift Dezire. The company has to differentiate between the variants promptly and perfectly. A person who wants to buy an Alto would know the limitation of the product. The person who prefers a high end model would definitely like to have the differentiation explained for the extra cost he is paying for the high end product. As a great sage would say, a person participating in formula one race cannot contemplate a car with 800 cc capacity instead of Ferrari.

Similarly a customer knows to distinguish between a normal branded car and a Rolls Royce. He knows how these two variants of different companies meet his requirement. He may prefer normal brand for some purpose and Rolls Royce for some other purpose.

Just as a customer prefers to have SB account with a foreign bank, just as a customer wishes to have an high end model of same car manufacturer and just as a customer wants to differentiate between two companies, Banks should create product folder to suit the high end customer and low end customer.

Thus the product positioning strategy takes care of satisfaction, utility; brand value and customer delight into account before implementation.

When a giant public sector bank came out with millennium bonds the timing was not considered proper. Foreign banks and some other private banks had covered the customers sufficiently in advance. Why no lower cadre officials in marketing department had not thought of the timing? Or whether such suggestions were given at all by the junior executives or they were just trying to appease the top management by simply nodding their heads. In public sector, junior executives, especially in the cadre of AGM and DGM only want to appease their top brass and they do not express any negativity even if they knew them for sure. Truth told by any one whether superior or junior or the lowest cadre is truth. Great people acknowledge such timing mistakes or wrong ideas. If it was not done, then the new form of lifts (outside glass cabin) in malls and shopping complexes would not have come into existence avoiding wasting of area.

Fatty salaries, Changing psychology in spending behavior and changing life styles have made the requirement of new products in the monetary sector. Foreign banks have been too quick to understand this and design new products and position them to attract the early catch. Cash back offer by Card companies are the best examples and more so the utilization of such schemes by foreign banks. Except one major public sector bank, no other public sector bank has used this cash back offer effectively. Again it is the product positioning strategy that has played a major role. Promotional mix of products is also part of product positioning strategy.

In Banking sector base rate plays major role. The base rate of various banks would set up a price differential to the customers. Giant public sector bank's base rate might be comfortably lesser than an ordinary public sector bank. Then the price difference comes. Still customers are available to all banks. How this is possible. It is by positioning the product with different rates like combo rates, differential processing charges, quick disposition, easy terms, concessional processing or zero processing charges, added insurance benefits and above all exemplary customer service.

27

Shifting customers across various channels is also a marketing tool

"The prime aim of any bank's management is how to manage crowd and identify the real customers of the bank."

Cost efficiency of distribution channels and expense management has a great bearing on the profitability for banks. Banks and customers assess the benefits of various distribution channels often. Cost efficiency and avoiding unprofitable products and services are the focus of many of the banks. The most cost efficient systems should be analyzed and customers should be engaged in such cost effective systems to the maximum extent possible. The expenses framework is formed by taking into consideration the elements of expenses involved say communication expenses like leased line expenses, call centre expenses, electronic equipments investment etc. **One of the "P"s of marketing is the Process.** Standard systems and procedures, customization of products and services and making different channels of services available to customers are few of the tasks of any marketing department.

The prime aim of any bank's management is how to manage crowd and identify the real customers of the bank. There are some public sector banks in south whose offices would look like ration shops with huge crowds thronging the doors in the initial week of any month. There are some public sector banks who want business in government schemes and priority sector schemes. This is one way of risk mitigation in decent words or in sharper comment it is avoiding decisions. Thus a healthier crowd may not be present in the bank's premises because only small loans as per government's schemes and small services like pension service, PPF service and populist services are extended. Thus it becomes the headache of any bank to push the crowd from the bank premises to different channels like ATM, POS terminal and internet banking. The crowd is pushed from bank premises to ATM centers, Malls and shopping centers and finally to their homes by making them to use internet banking service. Customers are segmented based on their behavior, requirement and category (industrial, personal, agricultural etc). Cost reduction on various channels is the main concern of the banks now. While shifting the customers, they should not feel that they are shifted from the bank branch. Cash back schemes on Debit and Credit Cards is one such attempt. Similarly, discounts on spending on POS terminals are also a marketing tool for shifting the crowd from the branches to various channels. In today's scenario banks are contemplating to use various social media for shifting the customers from bank branch. **Place, Promotion and Physical Evidence are other three "P" of Marketing.** These are also involved while shifting the customer from one channel to other.

Lots of promotional programs in Debit card/Internet banking and credit card transactions are examples of promotion and even identity for Physical Evidence. These elements when rightly mixed and used turn out to be an excellent marketing tool.

Banks should use various distribution policies and differential pricing together. They should understand the key concepts and samples related to distribution. Customer's choice of channel of distribution, their day to day issues on such channels, clarity of information on such channels, level of market exposure of such customers should all be studied by the bank. By ascertaining the market share of the ATM users, Internet banking users and credit card users through the MIS department, the bank should announce various concessions, promotional activities and facilities for the customers to choose the channel. It is to be understood that the various other channels like ATM, Net Banking, POS work out cheaper for the bank than to serve the customer through the branch. "P"s are to be judiciously identified and used along with an integrated marketing plan. Channel conflict should be avoided. If not avoided should be identified, clarified and answered to. The marketing team in entirety should be taught of the channel qualities and customer reaction to these channels for avoiding conflicting issues.

Every channel has got a life for the customer. A customer who is regular visitor to the branch will after great prompting by the branch marketing official shift his channel from branch to any other channel say e banking, debit card usage or POS usage. The customer will stay there in such channels as long as he is convinced about its simplicity and it usefulness. Once he gets a doubt and discomfort in such channel he would either try to shift to another channel for another try or will shift to branch itself. Banks should play a major role in making such customers to stay as long as possible in such alternate channels. If he is not convinced with any of the channels then quite naturally he will shift his loyalty to other Bank. Environmental factors, frauds, phishing activities play a major role in channel diversification or reverting from the channel to basic banking.

28

Segmentation, targeting and positioning – An understanding

"It will be better if the MIS department wisely groups customers into various segments and update the same periodically and pass on the information to the marketing department for applying the marketing tools".

Public sector bank per se does not indulge in segmentation, targeting and positioning in real terms. However they do it differently. Generally bank's business is divided into Deposits, Advances, Third party products/services and other normal banking services.

Deposits are classified as deposits from public, institutions, government and non government. They are further classified as current account and savings account and term deposits. In all these the interest rate plays a vital role based on the requirement to pay to the customer when needed. All Banks maintain Asset Liability Matching system and the deposits are classified into different time buckets so as to make use of the funds collected in the best profitable way. The term spread will be used to identify the profitable margin available to the banker after paying out the interest and other normal incidental charges.

Similarly Advances are segregated as Core advances, Priority advances including Agricultural advances, Retail advances, Forex advances, Industrial credit and SME credit and so on. The pricing of all these advances are done according to the base rate every bank is operating with. Earlier it used to be BPLR or prime lending rates. The entire amounts available for lending to various segments are to be apportioned to such segments only by the top management. Each segment will have its own advantage and disadvantage. Depending upon the risk involved the profitability will be decided. So far the highest profit segment has been credit card segment followed by retail segment. In one of the South based PSB, retail segment had helped very much the bank to turn around and also increase the profitability. Many of the PSBs have concentrated on retail banking with various attractive schemes. Similarly during the crucial time of turn around for a south based public sector bank, it was the investment department which showed the glimpse of profit for the year.

At this juncture only the market share, penetration and marketing strategy would come into play. A good public sector bank should select a good tool of market analysis for survival. It will be better if a system of **Marketing Audit** is introduced by these banks. General marketing concepts will be useful for the segment wise products. This is applicable as long as the customer is in the industrial civilization age. Today the customer has shifted from industrial civilization age to tech savvy age or cloud computing age which is also called wisdom age. Neo marketing concepts and techniques are to be used to retain customers into our fold. In earlier days **managerial decision making** was sufficient to conduct business. But today's parlance it is only "**marketing decision making**" which is the key word.

Role of information system plays a significant part in today's banking activities. Marketing decision making through introduction of general marketing concepts is envisaged by PSBs. MIS department has to provide correct information to marketing department for achieving best results. Recently one of the Public Sector Banks introduced a special discount card by tying up with a big hospital. The discount cards were to be given to the customers with a particular level of deposits with the bank. Probably the MIS department would have given the data to marketing/development department. But after issue of cards lots of complaints and grievances surfaced because MIS department had not taken the total multiple deposits but had taken total single deposit. This appeared to be discrimination to some of the customers, since they had the necessary deposit amount with the bank but not as one bulk deposit but as three or four deposits. This biggest disadvantage is for the marketing department or the branch manager who is also forming part and parcel of marketing team. The customer would directly pounce upon the BM to know the reason for the differential treatment. Even though reasons can be singled out for selecting the recipients, there will be total dissatisfaction with the customers on the whole. Thus MIS department plays a major role in segmenting and applying marketing concepts. It has to convince top management about the methods of segmentation and its effects.

Data received from the MIS department should help marketing department to target the product to audience for better marketability. Targeting the right customer with the right product will always bear a better result. Mixing of products and differential pricing of products is also done on the basis of information from MIS department. It is the duty of MIS department to correctly give the requisite data to marketing department for effective implementation of the marketing policies. For any product **4 factors** are important. **One is production** of the product, **two is marketing** of the product and **three is selling** of the product and **four the final and utmost important factor is the customer called as target or audience**. It is a cakewalk for any organization which has target audience to sell its products. That is why third party products were introduced in Banks. It will be better if the MIS department wisely segments different customers into various segments and update the same periodically and pass on the information to the marketing department for applying the marketing tools.

29

Innovation is not possible?

"More Time taken by the customer at your site does not mean that it is impressive but reveals that there is dearth of information in your website. It means that your bank is unable to give the required information to the customer promptly."

Innovation is a marketing tool. Pungent copying right from letter heads, notes, RFPs, sites, etc are the bane of public sector banks. Is not innovation possible? If so why is it not tried? If one observes, there will be resemblance between the internet, intranet portals, and advertisement panels, colour selection for the name boards, logos, and their meanings and more especially in the approach itself. Recent developments like Face Book pages, special portals like marketing or wealth management may all be similar. Branding and conducting melas or campaigns are similar.

Even though similarities are there a lot can be understood from these communication tools. A person visiting the site of a public sector bank stays for quite a long time. It is the misconception of tech department that the visitor is more interested in the site of the bank. But in real terms it is not so. The customer is unable to get the required details and that is why surfing the site to get such details. The site management team should try to understand the real intention of the customers surfing the site. In certain cases the smart tech department junior executives boast to their top management that customer wants to stay for longer time with their site than other bank's site.

In some of the foreign bank's site the search mechanism is typical. If you give the search word as home loan it leads you conveniently to the right page wherein you get all the required details for home loan along with the contact details of the agents or officials. In public sector bank's site it may not be so sharp but probably it will lead to loan portfolio then to personal banking and then to home loan. More Time taken by the customer does not mean that your site is impressive but reveals that there is dearth of information in your website. It means that your bank is unable to give the required information to the customer promptly.

Innovative Web Site visibility is another factor which attracts customers. Analyzing the customer interest and designing the site, analyzing the site activity properly, extending facilities through site promptly, making it functional, seamless and continuous will be best policy. Sporadic updating of information to satisfy the top brass of bank, not updating the site with the day to day changes which may be reflected in the intranet of the bank (with that only many front line staff and call centre staff give particulars to the customers) and holding stale schemes on the portal are all factors weakening the bank's image.

In many of the sites of the public sector banks very important details would not be available. While designing the site proper planning would not have been done. In one of the PSB site information about the branches dealing forex business or dealing government business like PPF savings account was not available for quite long time. It was reported that in spite of repeated requests no efforts were taken by the technology department to update such data. In some of the sites even data regarding branches would be missing. One serious complaint about the sites is non availability of basic data like IFSC code, basic banking charges, customer educative details etc correctly. Similarly many NRI customers have felt the difficulty with the PSBs in knowing the method of remittance, in knowing when the funds will reach the beneficiary, whether funds have reached beneficiary under foreign remittance and who should be contacted for a responsible reply. Many a times even the mandatory details may not be updated in the sites.

30

Minimum pyramid hierarchy

"The performance of the lower officer would not be brought to the knowledge of the top executive by the junior executive like AGM or CM since he will be showing the same in his performance appraisal report. Also such executives would be saying on a later period that they had only performed the task by themselves."

Technology department, Corporate Communication department and Marketing department should come under the same Administrative head either ED or CMD. As explained earlier Tech department is the real villain for the marketing department. Any Bank would steer forward wherever there is coordination between the marketing department and the technology department.

Technology department might want to put certain data in the website to appease the top brass about some of the schemes or products for which basic functionalities are not yet made ready. Marketing department would proceed canvassing the customers for such activity. When the customers come forward to avail such facility, the facility would not be ready. Similarly when marketing team sells a product or service and there is some dearth of service or issues, Technology should give full support to their team. In many public sector banks when the marketing team would have sold tech savvy products for which queries arose, there would not be support from technology team. The marketing department would only face the wrath of the customers.

Marketing department has the responsibility to induct new products, conduct market surveys and bring product innovation based on customer feedback. In public sector most of the officials of any cadre are not customer centric but executive centric. Whatever top executives say that alone would be executed. Also everyone would like to catch the attraction of the top executives. In the process officials especially in the cadre of junior executives like AGM would vie with each other for competition to catch the eyes or glimpse of the top executive. In the process the marketing man would deny the product or service suggested by Technology Man and technology man would chide the product or service suggested by the marketing team. Intelligent Tech department executives would strike down the request of the marketing team initially and stealthily release the same product or service at a later time without marketing team's knowledge. By the time marketing team makes any representation, already damage would have been done to it and the tech team would have achieved the credit. Competition in this does not stop with AGM level but spread to senior executive like GMs even. My friend from one of the PSBs was telling a funny story. The senior most executive of another department was announcing the feat achieved by marketing junior executive as the achievement of his amidst executives wherein the top executives were also present and gained huge applause. Such jokes have been happening in all banks and to avoid such unpleasant things it is better to bring these two departments at least under one head so that there would be perfect co ordination and no foul play is possible.

This game not only stops with the higher level executives but also with lower officers too. There is one performance appraisal formality with these public sector banks in which the officials have to bring their achievement. Top level officers might claim performances of the lower ranking officers as their achievement in their appraisal. The appraisals would be done at various stages. A scale one or two officer will be reviewed by CM or AGM. A CM or AGM would be reviewed by higher executive like DGM or GM. The performance of the lower officer would not be brought to the knowledge of the top executive by the junior executive like AGM or CM since he will be showing the same in his performance appraisal report. Also such executives would be saying on a later period that they had only performed the task by themselves. To avoid all these things at least for marketing department and technology department all performance appraisals should be done by GM levels jointly so that the lower level executives will not eat away the sweat of the junior officers.

It will be welcome if a joint training is arranged for both tech department and marketing department officials then and there. Understanding practically and theoretically the managerial marketing decision making process and general marketing concepts by both teams will lead to a smooth functioning. This will help both the teams to understand how to formulate marketing plans and understand the sequential stages within the marketing planning process. They should be able to appreciate the integrated nature of the plans and technology involved. Understanding of the marketing budgets, schedules of activities, responsibilities, implementation, supervision, control and audit done jointly by both the departments will improve the business. It should also be remembered that a contingency plan is always kept ready for action by the joint team.

The seamless movement of info among the cells/departments and the clear understanding of the role of each cell/departments are vital requirements. Clear documentation of the roles and responsibilities of the cells/department is required.

It will be in the interest of the bank management to keep proper job descriptions for each level of executive management. This will go a long way to avoid duplication in reporting of an activity at two levels.

"If the language is not correct what is said is not what is meant.

If what is said is not what is meant what ought to be done remains undone. Appreciate, accept, acknowledge and reconcile to the requirements.

31

What are the missing links in public sector?

"Formal marketing research should be started by all PSBs at least starting from extraordinary, very large branches or metro/urban branches."

"Concern for the customer and his requirements should be the chief purpose of all marketing endeavours."

Smooth marketing activity requires good and solid CRM data which is mainly lacking in most of the public sector banks. Funniest part of the game is about information sharing amongst marketing officers of various banks that some banks have invested in CRM package without even having CRM data of customers. If it is true then it is really pathetic. How can the software work without data? In the present scenario there are plenty of secondary data available through service providers. But primary data availability cannot be confirmed by most of the banks. Even if data are available the correctness of data cannot be taken for granted. Public sector should understand the difference between primary and secondary data and should be able to appreciate how such data can be used to hone up business and marketing decisions. The banks should locate the main sources of these data for effective operation of CRM software. Credible CRM data plays a role of information in marketing decision making. Formal marketing research should be started by all PSBs at least starting from extraordinary, very large branches or metro/urban branches. The data of all the customers should be somehow collected at least through outsourcing process and this data should be made available to the counter staff when a customer reaches the counter. The staff should be able to know whether he can sell any third party product and any other regular banking products, insurance or mutual fund products so that the meaning of financial super market would be met. Also the customer will not try to go to other bank in search of such product.

Initiating data collection that too correct data collection would mean starting of formal marketing research methodology which is vital stage in marketing research process. This is undoubtedly a new concept and is easily not getting into the minds of the stake holders. But it should be done at any cost. Even software institutions would be willing to cooperate in these issues at least for the sake of selling their CRM software. Collection of data of the customers is the fundamental step for data base marketing. Many SMS service providers and email operators have started somehow collecting secondary data and approach banks for sharing them as marketing tool. Should not banks try to get their data of their own customers?

MARKETING, THE SACROSANCT MANTRA

Human revolution has seen agrarian age, industrial age, computer age and now they are on communication age which is otherwise called wisdom age. Today the space available for reaction is very short and may further develop to nano seconds. Presently web based marketing, communication based marketing are fast developing. Social media and innovative web technologies are profusely used (day on day) to bring more customers into the fold of banks. Many public sector banks have started peeping into areas like face book, twitter etc to take advantage of the latest technology. They are yet to make significant efforts to reach customers through technology.

Mundane activities would no longer hold good in public sector banks. Corporate Communication department would sanction a sponsorship because of political and or bureaucratic pressure from the top. They would inform marketing department to put up a stall just because they had given the sponsorship. In real sense such stalls would not have even a single visitor. Many banks also would hesitate to utilize the opportunity to encash the situation. They would not spend further on such stalls and attract the crowd. The crowd might not also be concerned about the stalls. Some sports activities in some of the metros in which public sector insurance companies and banks have sponsored heavily had stalls from these public sector organizations. However whether any marketing activity was possible? It would be always a question mark.

Today internet based techniques are developing. All public sector banks should start pioneering in this field and deploy young staff for these activities. Having recruited MBAs, that too from very big institutions, asking them to sit at the counters to print pass book would amount to only mockery. These young generation bankers should be asked to popularize the new technologies the 21st century is going to witness. Banking activities have gone global. ATM cards, Credit cards, accounts operational through global communication systems throw open great opportunities to the PSBs. These facilities should be tried out and used by the public sector banks to stay in competition with the private sector giants. There are issues of frauds on credit cards and ATM cards without the knowledge of the customers. The gullible poor public share their secret codes and CVV numbers to the fraudsters. Banks have to use their intellectuals who had been specially recruited for redressing these issues.

Concern for the customer and his requirements should be the chief purpose of all marketing endeavours. The PSU banks should not miss it in the midst of the routine mundane activities.

An independent marketing department with the right type of employees, junior and senior executives with the domain freedom to pursue the right type of value adding products and services is the missing link.

32

Can SERVQUAL and GAP model help public sector?

"It should be remembered by any bank that the depositors' interest is more supreme and prime than the loan customers, because their fund is only being lent to these takers. When there is default from this segment, then the depositors' interest is ultimately affected."

"Even when the customer's requirements are properly brought to the notice of the top team, there may be dearth of service or performance which should be addressed to. This requires committed workforce from the management."

Marketing is associated with service quality and any dearth of service would speak on the performance of marketing team. It is high time that the marketing boss looked into the features offered by the above models to improve service quality. It would be better if the following aspects are taken care of by the marketing team as a whole.

Servqual concept highlights the main components of high quality service. As it is envisaged any marketing activity flourishes only when best quality is assured in any product or service offered to a customer. More so in banking scenario quality means prompt customer service. Public sector banks should analyze all the GAPs and cement the inadequacies that affect performance.

Management should correctly perceive what the customers want through quality marketing research activity. Customer's expectations should be properly interpreted by the marketing team on the field. What is demanded by the customers should be brought to the knowledge of top management without filtering at the lower levels. There should be perfect connectivity from the front line to the top boss.

Even when the customer's requirements are properly brought to the notice of the top team, there may be dearth of service or performance which should be addressed to. This requires committed workforce from the management. Service details should be clearly established. Managements should look into newer areas of service.

Another area which reveals dearth of service is quality of staff. Unions attempt to extend promotions to own staff at all cadres. Sub ordinate staffs who are promoted should be properly trained. Similarly when the Award staff (clerks) gets promoted to officer cadre there should be a mental change in their attitude and they should inculcate a paradigm shift in their behavior. Manual banking process underwent a change with the advent of total branch computerization and followed by core banking solutions. These transitions had been smooth enough. But sudden burst of branch opening has made branches devoid of staff. Mass retirements in the years 2015 onwards may affect the service in most of the public sector banks. Human resource policy itself undergoes a drastic change.

Over past two decades PSU banks had a squeeze on hiring. In spite of that many banks had gone for campus recruitment and recruited professionally qualified people from Universities and B schools. In the next two or three years there will be good number of people retiring from the PSBs and that is going to create a vacuum or going to be a crisis for the banks. Some of the banks have given chances for junior level people on a fast track mode to get promoted to higher cadre. It is a question mark whether such people were exposed to challenging projects. The same has happened in marketing department. When they newly recruited professionally qualified people for marketing department, they failed to put them on challenging projects or failed to provide them the decision taking power in implementing a new marketing strategy or activity for the PSBs. There is a comment that PSBs are a misfit in the world of Google, Facebook etc. The top level of these banks which had recruited the professional boys never gave a chance to these youngsters to apply their mind on various medium as face book or twitter with a free hand. Not only the compensation to these youngsters is less compared to private sector peers, the work freedom to these professionals is also zero. Top managements have been concentrating on Advance portfolio and other business matters. But they have not concentrated on the vacuum that is going to be created both in the field of HR management and Marketing management when sizeable senior staff would be retiring soon. It may be felt that the HR managements have miserably failed to estimate the exodus not only in HRM department but also in marketing department. Some Top CEOs who had migrated to apex level postings after brief stay in one or two PSBs have criticized that the quality and competence of people managing HR function saying that those HR executives had no expertise or training in HRM. Some have said that these HR executives have landed to their position by chance and not by a design or plan. During their tenure at least, the expertise of HRM department should have been revamped.

The next few years will be a difficult trajectory for the PSBs as a whole. The experienced staff has to be replaced. But replacing them with new recruits will not serve the purpose. Having recruited professionals, it is the duty of the PSBs to expose them to new projects and activities by giving them the necessary freedom and channelizing them into groove with the help of existing staff who have abundant expertise in banking activities. Bipartite settlements also add effect to that. There is tendency from a particular region people joining the work force in banking sector. Existences of sub ordinate cadre, clerical cadre and junior officer's cadre have undergone a vast change and one man branches are the order of the day. There appears to be a mismatch between demand and supply in work force. Internet based system of functioning is also making drastic changes among the working procedures. Persistent customer education and training on the newer technologies are not undertaken by many of the banks.

Marketing teams' members make high claims about the service level. Creation of customer relationship manager post in some banks has made dedicated workforce to attend to a group of high net worth customers. Marketing teams' claim and the service rendered by the branches should match. Otherwise there will be dissatisfied customers. Wrong communication would increase the expectations of the customers. Failure to perform as per team's assurances involves misunderstanding amongst customers.

Banks engage in fraud control measures, measures to protect customers' interest and introduce lots of controls for transaction done on line. Customer may not understand that these things are done to protect his own interest and may show their dissent. Out of the ten determinants at the least the determinants like competence, credibility, security, reliability and responsiveness should be attended to.

Similarly the **GAP model of service quality** also throws light on the coordination between the marketing team and various other heads. The main GAP between the expected service and perceived service plays a greater role in productivity. Management's perception of consumers' expectation should be properly communicated to the field personnel to reduce or eliminate the gap between the service standards and service delivery. Corporate communication's work flow, general customers' perception, marketing teams' image building and Branches' (ground force) performances all leave a level of expectation. The key contributory factors should be analyzed properly. Adequate market research orientation, improved upward communication and clear relationship focus would improve the marketing team's effort.

Another gap as noted earlier is the deficiencies in the HRM policies. Bank staff has no longer attachment to their job. They tend to go on VRS in many banks. Management's policies because of security reasons are unable to support the ground staff to a great extent. The same mistake done in private sector bank by ground level staff unknowingly or unintentionally, which is viewed leniently, is viewed seriously by the public sector bank. Supply and demand position of staff at various branches especially at the rural level that too in single man branches have led to frauds and that worries the work force to opt such places of postings. Sudden spurt in branch opening also leads to dissatisfaction to both customers and staff. With the modern marketing tools being introduced, management and engineering graduates being recruited from top institutions, internet based tech service increasing, it is logical that banks should resort to such new analysis tools for determining the service gaps which is part and parcel of marketing activity.

PSBs adopt different standards for fixing targets. South based banks have around 100 to 200 crores as target for Chief Manager level, as against 2000 to 4000 crores for the same level in the north based banks. Similar wide variation persists in targets fixed for Asst General Managers Deputy general Managers and General Managers. One of the marketing team mate used to share how in a south based bank, when the zonal head reached 9900 crore mark crackers were fired to celebrate the turnover. The same was done silently by a Senior manager or Chief manager in some other public sector bank. Bank Managements want more per employee business. **Have they concentrated on per executive business? There is a real gap between the functioning styles of various public sector banks**. That difference itself would bring lots of dissatisfaction between the customers and staff. In one of the powerful and top most public sectors' giant, customers would not be able to question the staff whereas in other PSBs the same customers would put the manager to embarrassments. Similarly there are some private sector giants who at times are heard to flout the rules which might not even attract the guardian bank's attention and action. For example when Government put pressure on the public sector banks to extend liberally educational loans, one of the south based bank was made a target by all and sundry. People used to threaten the branch manager that they would write to the concerned minister to mend him. The south based bank also extended extensively, it was revealed out in their press reports. In certain cases when the public approached the giant bank with the same tactics the bank did not bother its branch managers and naturally the pressure landed on the south based bank totally. It should be remembered by any bank that the depositors' interest is more supreme and prime than the loan customers, because their fund is only being lent to these takers. When there is default from this segment, then the depositors' interest is ultimately affected. One of the marketing team members used to share an incident how a watch and ward staff of the giant bank used to threaten the small bank staff while drawing pension through the bank. The reason was simple. The giant bank did not permit DA for his service in the bank as well his ex- military service. Hence he preferred his pension through the small PSB. When a knowledgeable Asst Branch Manager took up the case and informed the watch and ward staff that the matter would be reported to his parent bank and pension transferred, the watch and ward staff submitted to his guilt requesting no action. Similarly some of the officials of the guardian banks have always tried to bother the PSB staff by showing their authority even after retirement. The above revelations are to only high light that how different banks have different working atmosphere which is basically bearing relationship to marketing activities and ultimately on service.

33

What requires to be done in public sector bank?

"From ignorance we mistake.

Out of mistakes we learn.

Learning is a continuous process.

Let us believe in that and proceed from dependence to independence through interdependence. It is the relay team. The kick start is given by the marketing team. Rest follows."

The first and foremost thing is to see that both marketing and technology departments are under one superior head of department say ED or CMD. In public sector there is a general tendency from Technology department to stall the suggestions on product/service by marketing department. The reason is very simple. Technology department would like to show it as its own finding. In meetings with top executives, the executives of Technology department would quote the performances of marketing department as their own since they are giving technical support and thus they account for it.

Second important thing is to place the performance appraisal of the junior officers to senior level executives say directly to ED or CMD so that they would know who had done the performance. Generally the performance of the lower level officer is shown by the middle level executive especially AGM cadre as his own in his performance appraisal. If a job description mechanism is put in place wrong claims can be weeded out and those who indulge in such wrongful claims may be suitably warned against future growth prospects in the bank.

Thirdly, on promotion a marketing officer in the cadre of CM should be given a department/branch change (especially one who had not shown any big performance). A non performer in particular would spoil the entire department. He cannot motivate, perform and steer people. He would insist on only questioning the marketing team which would totally de-motivate the entire team. He will always try to trim the department since he cannot show per employee business.

Fourthly, marketing officers should not be used to do errands of the bank/branch. Left to himself any marketing executive would perform if not in first year, from second year onwards. Once he is asked to do errands, he becomes a slave and wants to oblige the local executive for survival. After two or three years he would know how to adjust to his boss, try to get a branch posting and shift away from marketing. Popular "Go for approach" of local executives would not motivate the marketing officer.

I would like to quote a lot from the revelations of Mr Stephen R Covey in the book "The 8th Habit – from effectiveness to greatness". Generations have crossed hunter/gatherer age, agrarian age, industrial age, information knowledge age and we are now on wisdom age. At each stage productivity has been multiplying in quantum and speed. He also observes that many of our modern management practices come from the industrial age. It gave us the belief that we have to control and manage people. This approach if handled today will alienate the employees, depersonalize work and create low trust among them. He quotes John Gardner's words like this. "Most ailing organizations have developed a functional blindness to their own defects. They are suffering not because they cannot resolve their problems, but because they cannot see their problems."

He also quotes that human beings are not things to be controlled in today's parlance, but are four dimensional –body, mind, heart and spirit. Any neglect in recognizing these four fundamentals makes a man a thing. In today's scenario of recruiting MBAs that too from IIMs and IITs if one does not follow Stephen R Covey's principles, then the result is going to be dissatisfying. He also quotes Buckminster Fuller as" All children are born geniuses, 9,999 out of every 10,000 are swiftly, inadvertently degeniusized by grownups.

He says between stimulus and response there is space. In that space lays our freedom and power to choose our response. In those choices lie our growth and happiness.

Fifthly, based on the above, the marketing official should be allowed to use the space arising from stimulus and response, action and reaction effectively to benefit him and as well the organization he belongs to. Trust is the key for all relationships. Great thinkers have said trust is the glue of organizations. Response time ie the space should be used by the marketing team on the whole and timely response and prompt response should be made possible. Any mismatch in response time and space usage leads to non performance.

His following quote, "The range of what we think and do is limited by what we fail to notice. And because we fail to notice that we fail to notice there is little we can do to change; until we notice how failing to notice shapes our thoughts and deeds." should be mantra of marketing department.

He quotes "The highest manifestations of four intelligences are: for the mental, **Vision**; for the physical, **discipline**; for the emotional, **passion**; and for the spiritual, **conscience**." He also says that vision; Discipline and Passion rule the word which is reality.

He also quotes Albert Schweitzer as saying, "In everyone's life, at some time, our inner fire goes out. It is then burst into flame by an encounter with another human being. We should all be thankful for those people who rekindle the inner spirit."

Finally I would like to quote my favourite statement from Mr Peter Drucker, "Doing things right is management and doing the right thing is leadership".

The top bosses of the public sector banks should look into four flavours namely Vision, discipline, passion and conscience with a deep thought. Management should think that we are no longer in industrial age or information knowledge age, but in wisdom age. Everything is easily commutable and communicable within split seconds. If that be the case with the **"things", then what about humans of present day.**

My final expectation from the public sector banks is as follows.

1. Let us differentiate between marketing and selling functions.

2. Let us define marketing vertical in real sense.

3. No management should neglect marketing department and order errands to be done by marketing team. They have some purpose.

4. Be tech savvy in the real sense.

5. Understand marketing function is all pervasive across the pyramid of organization. When you see per employee business, see also per executive business.

6. Marketing and Technology department should be under the same top boss.

7. PSBs should aim at formation of Marketing Concept, team, tools, strategy and implementation programme.

8. PSBs should concentrate on cost and price policy using market research.

9. Products should be defined in a finer and easier way.

10. Customer analysis, Customer relationship management should be done through the combined team of Marketing and Technology.

11. Over submissiveness to top brass spoils marketing plan.

Sachin mask on face does not make one Sachin.

From ignorance we mistake.

From mistakes we learn.

Learning is a continuous process.

Let us believe in that and proceed from dependence to independence through interdependence. It is the relay team. The kick start is given by the marketing team. Rest follows.

About the Author

"A marketing man should be agile, aggressive, affectionate, and astute to clinch any business."

When I finished my degree at St Joseph's College Tiruchirapalli, Tamil Nadu, in 1974, my ambition was to get only a job. Due to sudden ill health at the time of my pre degree schooling, I had to compromise on a science degree foregoing my ambitions I had in my mind. Since I had sufficiently scored in the pre degree exam I settled for a science degree with Chemistry Major – a branch of study which was in demand. All my friends had by then gone to Regional Engineering College- Tiruchirapalli, Tamil Nadu, IIT Chennai, Madras University or Medical Colleges at various places. During college days, there was a special course called "COSIP" meaning no gossip but as **Co**llege **S**cience **I**mprovement **P**rogramme. During college time that helped me to get my certificate course in Photography.

After finishing my college, I took up an agency for selling chemicals, washing powder, detergents and soap. I learnt the art of selling but then had not known anything about marketing. I did certain activities which might be called marketing activities but by then I had never known that to be an activity connected to marketing.

It was during the month of April, which fell parallel to the Tamil month "Chithirai", I took up my sales activity for a detergent powder. I had four members in my team and in the crowded city of Madurai, Tamil Nadu; we had taken permission in front of a shop to put our products for sale. That assumed the name "Spot Sales" and many tried to copy that method further. We used to add some complement to the detergent packet and sell it at the price at which the product would be available in the stores. Being enticed by the complement offered by us, many people purchased from us and it was easy for us to approach the shops after a week or so since the product was already known amongst customers and many customers had contacted the shops particularly asking for the complement. We had good reception from the shop owners as there were enquiries about our products. Very casually I had done that never knowing that it was a marketing technique. Similarly most of the shops wanted a good name for the products and never wanted an ordinary packing but insisted for a nice packing which I did and was successful. That time I had chosen very attractive names for my detergents and cleaning powder and I could easily compete with giants in the industry. All such attempts, I learnt later, were marketing techniques only. Due to some difficulties, I had to leave that business. With photography course I had done at St Joseph's college, Tiruchirapalli, Tamil Nadu, I joined as an industrial photographer as a non muster roll candidate in a public sector organization. I was first asked to join at a Factory in Tiruchirapalli, Tamil Nadu which was my native place; from there I was asked to go to Chennai (then Madras) and from Chennai I was taken to Maharashtra in a car by a gentle man whom later I came to know as Site- in- charge of a power plant. Thus, two days after leaving Tiruchirapalli I was landing in a remote Village in Maharashtra to work for that public sector organization which was working on a turnkey power project there.

I had lots of fun as a photographer and gained good experience. I had to work on heights since the erections used to happen at the top of engineering structure for power project. Incidentally, I was a committee member of Canteen. One day we were having committee meeting in the night around 10 which lasted till 11 o'clock. Suddenly the telephone in the room rang and there was a call for me. A fire broke out damaging a rotor worth few crores. I had to take photographs of the place along with the rotor to claim insurance. I put forth all my efforts on that night and presented the accident spot with the rotor through photographs. Insurance company had fully compensated my organization at the earliest. (Good presentation is the basic criteria of marketing)

After few days, I again received an S O S message asking me to report to site at an odd hour. A worker from Kerala had fallen from a height of 270 feet and was dead. I had to take the photographs of that event which sent jitters in my mind as I was also climbing tall structures to take photographs of erection of parts of turbo generator or chimney. I had decided to change my job.

In the meanwhile, I had received a message from my native place informing me of an appointment with a Public Sector Bank. I approached my boss who reluctantly agreed to relieve me. AGM/HRM organized a meeting for my relieving and it was a great moment in my life. When I had doubted that whether I would be relieved or not, I was not only relieved without hassles but was given great commendations on the work I had done on the above mentioned crucial occasions.

I joined bank and within four years I got the promotion opportunity but missed it because my confidential report to head office was not sent from my branch which was a formality at that time. Eventually, I did not get the promotion. By then, I had concentrated on more union activities. Having missed promotion, my life changed from that time onwards and I took to union activities too seriously. In almost all the cases I had represented, I could achieve grievance redressed for my members and I was respected by my colleagues. I was very friendly and could get on well with the executives. I was working in accounts section and was actively associated in union activities as a committee member for a long time.

It was then that I had met a gentleman who identified my marketing skills and that in turn changed my profile. The meeting with him started with a heated argument between us. That gentleman was elevated as Asst General Manager and on that occasion he had called for a meeting. He wanted to enforce discipline and while addressing the department staff, he said that all should work for the organization and there was no use of bringing external force like Union or Association to get things done to their advantage. He was quoting a story of Lord Emadharmaraja (who controls death and his decision is final) and ended the meeting with a note that everyone should quietly work without demur. He gave opportunity for all staff to express their views and no one came forward but I decided to venture. I welcomed his suggestion stating that our bank was undergoing a difficult phase but insisted that any work should be extracted in a friendly and persuasive manner and not in autocratic style. I purposely quoted the story of Sathyavan and Savithri in which the lady fought and won over the same Emadharmaraja and took back the life of Sathyavan. Everyone was perplexed including me. I thought I had exceeded my brief but nevertheless I was emphatic in the sense that I had truly represented my employees.

Later on that day evening my Executive called me and interacted with me. He was in all praise for me and said that he liked the way I had expressed myself. Initially I thought that he was mocking at me. But later I realized that he was a gentleman and throughout my career in the bank I had not seen such a Good Samaritan or gentleman in the executive cadre. He later left our bank and joined as a top level official in yet another bank.

While I reported to him as an officer, I exploited my marketing skills to achieve good business for the bank. He also supported me in all possible ways. It was then that all Private Sector Insurance companies had tied up with Public Sector Banks. I had an interaction with my boss and told him that a Public sector entering into an agreement with a Private sector was not good. He quietly replied, "Friend! Our parents have decided to remarry. If you are interested give your ashirwads (greetings) else get out of the organization. Remember that you have chosen to be an officer and you are no more a union man". It was at that time insurance products were introduced by all banks. Added to insurance products (both life and non life) mutual funds & gold coins were included and were known and bundled as Third Party Products. Many people were identified and trained for pushing these products to Bank's own customer. It was in this context only, the jargons like marketing and selling entered into banking area along with target and performance. Our zone had tall target since my Zonal Manager was highly regarded by the Top management. My ZM called me from the branch and gave me the pushing (marketing or selling) activity stating that he had confidence in my marketing (selling and convincing capability) skills. The target was almost 3 crores – a tall order for an incipient salesman. I had to accompany a branch manager to a big customer. I had planned in my own way. Immediately on meeting the MD of the organization, the branch manager told about the insurance product and wanted some policy to be taken for the sake of the bank. He had quoted in thousands as premium.

I had made a mental calculation while going in the car. Three crore premium was the target; If I sold premium of 10 lakhs per person then I had to catch hold of 30 parties. It meant that I should see potential prospects of at least 90 or 100 out of which 20 or 30 might be willing. In case I achieved 2 crores target as explained above for balance one crore I might have to approach clients who could be expected to give one lakh premium each, which might involve reaching out to 100 prospects at a hit rate of one out of ten prospects to be the buyer.

MARKETING, THE SACROSANCT MANTRA

Were it possible and whether all those people like administrative officers in Zonal Office and Branch Managers who were connected to this were aware of it?

When the manager had finished, he gave the lead to me. I started talking to that gentleman (MD of that organization) and was enquiring about his family members and the net worth of the gentleman. Then I deviated the topic, took the party on my stride and told him that based on his net worth and yearly income, he had to save at least 10 lakhs for each child per month. Hence for two children 20 lakhs and thus I arrived at a yearly premium of at least 2 crore minimum. I suggested him to pay the first premium by cash and further told him that he could open a yearly RD account with the branch so that the further premiums could be paid out of RD maturity.

The manager was perplexed and was pinching my thigh showing his disapproval. The party was more or less convinced about the saving concept but not with the premium amount but the manager was so confused and he thought that we were unnecessarily troubling the party. I quickly came out of the room and called my Zonal Manager and he responded. I gave a cinematic dialogue," If I close the deal, it is "X" amount and if you are doing it is five times of that amount." I told my ZM that I would get a premium of minimum 10 lakhs but if he comes we would get at least 50 lakhs.(even though I had pitched 2 crore premium.) He asked me to put the phone down and while I and my manager were talking to that party, suddenly, a figure crept in and I was astonished to see my ZM. We finished the deal and from that time onwards we learnt lots of clues in making strategies in both marketing & selling. I learnt at that moment only, the difference between marketing and selling. I realized, as part of marketing strategy, the importance of studying the surrounding, how to talk, present myself and my product. I learnt to evaluate my opponent also to decide the product which I would be able to sell to my opponent. **And finally, I understood the great fact that for any deal in third party products to be closed a third force is required between the seller and purchaser. The third force should have some influence, force and convincing ability over the buyer.**

Coimbatore is the industrial hub of Tamil Nadu, India having 'n' number of companies. I had an opportunity to meet the highest number of Managing directors of companies in my life. That gave me an extraordinary experience. It developed my personal skills. It gave me Perseverance, Patience, Passion which I deemed as three Ps of marketing man. I had met executives who could be dissolved within few seconds and few who would dissolve you and mentally upset you with the result you will run away from marketing career.

I had one such experience. I had to accompany a branch manager to a tough customer. Manager had already briefed me about the person and hinted that none of the marketing officers were able to make him talk. The customer's strategy was, if he opened his mouth, manager would definitely take some premium from him. Hence he decided not to open his mouth. I was accompanied by two more officers from marketing and the manager initiated the topic. My colleagues also interacted with him quoting lots of jokes and anecdotes. The gentleman never opened his mouth and was seriously seeing some accounts statement. I was going through the room and noted that he was manufacturing a unique product which if marketed properly would be certainly a hit. After few minutes manager showed me signs of disinterest. Then I started my dialogue with the customer. I just said that the products were extremely good and that they were unique. Then that customer lifted his head and exclaimed "Is it?" I promptly replied, "Yes Sir". I told him that the product was unique and would attract definitely all city hotels. I told him that he would get good name for it and some export market too. The gentleman slowly started opening up and interacted with me for quite some time. My manager was perplexed, probably he thought that he might be wasting his time and I was taking his time. My conversation extended and finally I could convince him to come out with some premium amount which was not bad. We all returned to the branch. Everyone was happy. Every one appreciated my move. **That was the time I learnt the art of reading opponent, his strength and weakness.**

A marketing man should be agile, aggressive, affectionate, and astute to clinch any business. I had won lots of rewards, awards, commendations and also scolding, admonishments & rebuke too. Later, I got promoted and posted to marketing department of Head Office.

www.ingramcontent.com/pod-product-compliance
Lightning Source LLC
Chambersburg PA
CBHW051520170526
45165CB00002B/541